C000163271

help**Less** - It is time to stop ⌐

To those who have the knowledge already

and are choosing to illuminate the path for others

and

To those who are waiting to shine their light

and

To those who don't know the light within exists yet

help**Less**

It is time to stop pleading
and start **leading**

Paula McCormack

helpLess - It is time to stop pleading and start **leading**

First published in 2011 by
Ecademy Press
48 St Vincent Drive, St Albans, Herts, AL1 5SJ
info@ecademy-press.com
www.ecademy-press.com

Printed and bound by Lightning Source in the UK and USA
Illustrations by Andrew Priestley
Set in Myriad and Warnock by Karen Gladwell
Design by Michael Inns

Printed on acid-free paper from managed forests. This book is
printed on demand, so no copies will be remaindered or pulped.

ISBN 978-1-907722-32-5

CONTENTS

PREFACE

If you have taken the time to pick this book up, like me, you probably have a great interest in people and in helping them to be the best they can be. From as far back as I can remember I have known that my purpose in this life was to help people. It sounds trite really and perhaps even pathetic because essentially all of us are here to help one another and contribute to this world we share.

What I have come to learn in my lifetime of serving this purpose is that there are ways that we can help that do genuinely move a person forward towards ownership of their life. And there are ways of helping that give another absolutely no reason to take any form of ownership for themselves or others. And there is also everything in between.

I have grown up around martyrdom and have observed its destructive yet compelling nature. I have been a product of it and I have exercised it, both with and without consciousness. I've been a passive and active observer of the helping society that we have built and what I see around me now, frightens me to an extent unimaginable.

Each day I experience people who believe that life is done to them and they are but mere passive recipients to it; to Government; authority; the economy; the environment; the weather; their boss; their family; their duty and obligations and so on and so on, the list is endless. I call these people, 'the waking dead'. They take no ownership or responsibility for themselves and for the most part are unaware of this fact. They have never been encouraged to do so, or shown that it is possible.

This is the society that we have come to know. This is the society that we are all responsible for building. This is the society that will lead humanity to implode upon itself. This is the society that will and has given all its power away to the few, who at free will, can and do take advantage when and wherever possibly for self-interest, consciously or unconsciously.

This is not a society I want to live in and doubtless if you're reading this, is it one that you want to live in either? I do not believe it is utopian, idealistic or quixotic to want to live in a society where people take ownership of their own lives and are self-determining within it. Where the concept of equality does not need to exist and where we are encouraged to explore the inner strength and beauty that lies within each of us and express that in a way that serves humanity.

In general our understanding of what it means to help has become distorted and paradoxically our actions in helping are serving to destroy, disempower and suppress society.

I realise this may sound somewhat far-fetched, however, if you are reading this I do not need to influence you to believe what I am saying. Inherently you already know something is not congruent, perhaps you've articulated it as I have, or differently. Or perhaps it is on the tip of your tongue but the words have not quite formed a coherent sentence yet. Or maybe just because you have an interest in people and are leading an organisation that has a social purpose you want to understand more of what you can do to fulfil your organisation's purpose.

I wrote this book because I am passionate about helping people in a way that enables their own power of self to be ignited and enlightened. I am extremely clear in making my distinctions of what help is and is not and I want to share my experiences and knowledge to ignite and enlighten more people. The more that understand these distinctions the greater and more purposeful our work in society can be. In turn we can begin to build communities that truly care for one another in a way that is mutually beneficial to all humanity.

Over decades I have been working with some of the most formidable leaders of social causes and with people in general who have woken up to life and the part they play within it. I have learned so much from every single person I have ever worked with and have taken great heed of all these learnings.

My personal life journey has been filled with challenges, opportunities, and traumas, all of which have brought with them both great joy, and pain. I use every morsel of these experiences to learn, develop, evolve, share and role-model. In this book I will share with you some of the more intimate details of these experiences and how I have used them to develop the thoughts, ideas, and tools that enable me in my work, so that you can take what you need of it and apply it in a way that is useful to you and for you.

Whilst the book focuses primarily on the UK, the observations are western society generic and can be found in general in any country, state or community within. However, the learnings contained can be applied universally in any society so wherever in the world your work takes you, there is much learning to be gained from within these pages and I encourage you to share its contents wide and far.

To offer this learning in a cohesive manner I have structured the book into three parts. The first part gives context for the remainder of the content, focusing upon what is meant by dependency and how we have come to create and perpetuate it throughout societal structures such as the welfare system. Further I take a look at how we organise the delivery of services in society, through sectors such as community and voluntary, public, and social enterprise and how we fund this. Finally in this part I define the role that leaders in these sectors play and how this is the key to building a society of the future, my utopian ideals!

Part two offers insight into human psychology and what makes us so unique yet so alike. This considers behaviour, emotions, conditioning, genetics and personal experiences and how we can use these studies to better understand how we have come to develop the society we now live in and in this understanding start to look at our role as helpers in society in a new light.

Finally part three presents The Adaptive™ approach which is the culmination of my life's work brought together to offer practical tools and ways in which we can build a society, that promotes empowerment, ownership, encouragement, love and life, and calls for immediate and deliberate action to bring this about – are you up for the challenge?

Before reading on I would ask that open your heart and mind, let there be no inhibitors to your consumption. Let the contents land wherever they land for you and allow yourself to fully experience their effect and impact. Be mindful of what immediately connects with you, what engages you, what incites and delights you, what angers you and what gives you renewed or newfound hope. And finally what insights can you bring to bear in your world that will truly make the difference to the difference you know you can deliver, what you were born to bring to bear in this life.

ACKNOWLEDGEMENTS

In my lifetime every single person I have ever met or observed has contributed to facilitating my writing of this book. So on the broadest possible scale I would like to thank humanity for what it teaches me in every moment of every day.

To all of the people who I have met in the course of my work who have taught me everything they know by just being, which allows me to now share this knowledge with you.

For all the many friends and colleagues who have, without reservation, guided, facilitated and supported me on this journey and those who pushed, cajoled and challenged. For all of you thank you for your feedback, opinions, directions and courage.

And those with a specific role, who include: Claire Charlton for extracting from within me all that I do and how I do it, facilitating the birthing of the Adaptive™; Helen Laverick, Kim Newman, Alison Stanners and John Walker for reading my drafts with such attention and intention; David Pilkington who proof-read again and again and offered additional insights; Andrew Priestley for his interpretation and subsequent creation of illustrations; Warm Design for developing the diamond; Triumphant and my co-colleagues (specifically Francis Hunt) on the 'Key Person of Influence' course; Christina Hall for enabling me to fully appreciate the depth and energetic value of our words; and finally Mindy Gibbins-Klein for providing structure.

For the leaders who gave of their time and of themselves to be interviewed in research for this book who include: Jeremy Gilley of Peace One Day; Cormac Russell of Nurture

Development; Keith Lorraine of Isos Group and Julie Kelly of Gentoo Group. Along with those there were also contributions from Jennifer Flint and Claire Sorensen as well as many others who responded to questions posted on different social media websites.

On an even more personal note thank you to my sister for her unyielding belief and my closest friends who provided me with love and encouragement at exactly the right times.

And finally a future thank you to all those of you who read, acknowledge, recognise, accept, share and take action to create a world where all humans cohabit in harmony, grace and love.

help**Less**

PART ONE

The Welfare State Creates and Perpetuates Dependency

It is time to stop pleading and start **leading**

CHAPTER ONE

Dependency

"Give a Man a Fish,
Feed Him For a Day.

Teach a Man to Fish,
Feed Him For a Lifetime."

Lao Tzu

Every person on earth is dependent. The extent to which we are though varies massively. No matter how self-sustaining or independent we believe we are, we are also paradoxically, by our very nature as humans, dependent. And most of what we're dependent upon are factors that are outside of our control, hence dependency is born.

So what does dependency really mean? Well it's a state of relying or being controlled, hence the factors will be outside our control.

So for example fishermen and farmers to a great extent are reliant (dependent) upon the weather. A health professional will be reliant upon people being ill or wishing to improve their health. Funeral directors are reliant upon people dying. Social landlords depend on having tenants in their properties. A shop relies on people buying their products. A charity relies on having clients that they can serve, and the average person relies upon another for love and support.

Dependency therefore can also be seen as an addiction all humans experience. We all need to be needed in some way as no man is an island and as humans we do not thrive when isolated from others.

Reflection Time

*No man is an island entire of itself; every man
is a piece of the continent, a part of the main;
if a clod be washed away by the sea, Europe
is the less, as well as if a promontory were, as
well as any manner of thy friends or of thine
own were; any man's death diminishes me,
because I am involved in mankind.
And therefore never send to know for whom
the bell tolls; it tolls for thee.*

John Donne

It is this craving to be connected to others that promotes and provokes a dependency that is both useful and less than useful in our lives.

Deeper in the structure of dependent though lies the following:

De   = *down, away or from*

Pend   = *hang, pen or confine*

Dent   = *an appreciable effect, often a lessening
                or adverse effect*

So if we put that together dependent takes on a whole new meaning that is a force that holds us down, adversely effecting and confining.

And it's this definition that this book aims to understand in the context of how we have run and managed our country through a welfare and social system that has promoted a greater and deeper dependency than was ever intended or imaginable. It is time to shift.

Cause and/or Effect

In my line of work facilitating people's development, everyday I hear the immortal words

"I can't"

And those saying it have no idea of the impact or power those two little words have on them. What I've come to notice is the physiology of the individual as the words come out of their mouth. Generally it's with eyes down, shoulders stooped, little body movement, sighing, a low tone (or for some a very loud tone). Overall energy is low, emotions are high and their mind is racing ten to the dozen with all the reasons why they are simply not good enough, and therefore can't. They've run this dialogue before and they know what it feels like to them. A resignation that whatever, is elusive to them, beyond them somehow and too far out of their personal reach.

I come from the Henry Ford school of thinking on this one: *"Whether you think you can or you can't, you are usually right."*

Henry Ford also said: *"I have not discovered that anyone knows enough to say definitely what is and what is not possible."*

Yet everyday billions of people say, think and truly believe they can't. But what makes them believe this? One answer is their conditioning. Yet two people can have exposure to exactly the same conditions and respond very differently. Think for just a moment, if you have siblings. Is their recollection of their childhood the same as yours? If you don't have siblings, think about your classmates at school. Was their experience of a teacher the same as yours? Probably not in both cases.

So is conditioning the answer? Well it's certainly not the full story but without doubt does have a profound effect.

In Action

In a previous career as a HR Manager I recruited an 18 year old boy (I'll call him Tom) to work in a food factory. The company employed 1,500 people, 90% of which were female and of the 10% that were male, most worked either in management or in engineering/IT positions.

On a temporary contract with the offer of permanent employment once he proved himself, Tom worked extremely hard. He fitted in with ease making great banter with the women and allowing himself to be nurtured by them, as well as being the butt of many jokes. Tom took it all in jest and as a 'happy-go-lucky' character he made friends quickly, learned even quicker and within six weeks the overwhelming desire of all those he worked with, and indeed myself as the recruiter, was that he was without doubt worthy of a permanent position (albeit part-time). On giving Tom this news, he told me this was the sign that he had become a man and he was so proud of his achievement. He told me he believed this was just the start of a whole new life for him, he said he felt free.

A few days later I saw Tom entering work. His face was battered and bruised. He walked slowly and I sensed with a very heavy heart. He would not speak to me or anyone else. A day later Tom collapsed at his station and was taken to the occupational health nurse. He asked to see me still refusing to speak. We found a quiet place and eventually he spoke. What he said shocked me to my core and at the same time somewhere else within me I was unsurprised.

Tom's father had beaten him because he was so ashamed of his son. He was ashamed on so many levels that Tom could not comprehend. Firstly he was working with a bunch of women, secondly in a factory, packing. Thirdly, and this was the cruncher for his dad. Tom was working!

You see, Tom had come from a long line of males who had not worked. Women had worked but only to provide 'pin money' to add to the benefits that the men got. Most of the women worked in the well-established factory that Tom now found himself in, with the wives, sisters and daughters of the men that Tom's dad considered to be his friends and comrades in adversity.

Tom's father was confused. His confusion led to anger and his anger led him to lash out at Tom and issue him with an ultimatum that he could either pack in the job and be like every other 'normal' man in his community or he could continue with the job but be excommunicated from the community and fend for himself.

Physically we fixed Tom up. Emotionally I did what I could to help him understand his father and how his actions were based on his 'love' for his son.

Ultimately, however, Tom left because in his words:
"I can't fend for myself and I don't want to lose my family."
He believed his only option was to pursue the life his father
deemed to be appropriate for him.

Without doubt, conditioning matters, beyond conscious awareness it matters a lot but it's not the full story.

So another option is programming.

We are born pre-programmed with instincts of survival and inbuilt within our brains we have a trigger for fight or flight. We also have instincts, or run the programmes that connect us with other humans. As babies we instinctively know when we are hungry, wet, uncomfortable, ill etc. These are all pre-programmed in us.

According to research conducted by Dr Bruce Lipton in his book 'Spontaneous Evolution' between the ages of zero and two, our brains operate only in delta mode, which is the slowest possible brainwave, meaning that operation only occurs in the unconscious mind. Through this mode there is a greater sense of empathy and intuition yet a decreased sense of awareness.

At two the waves speed up a little and from then until the age of about six, the child moves to a theta state. These are the brainwaves of REM sleep, which is in the border between the unconscious and conscious state. In this state, the mind is capable of deep and profound learning, healing and growth which is everything we see in a toddler and a child up to the age of six. You will have heard the saying "children are like sponges soaking everything up".

From the age of six to twelve we move into the Alpha state, a higher wave again yet still in a state of relaxation that is associated with creativity and tremendous learning.

It is not until we reach the age of twelve that we move into the full consciousness of Beta waves, where thinking, decision making, judging, problem solving and actioning dominate our waking moments. Which conversely is also the point at which most adolescence also commence puberty. And we wonder why they appear as a different species!!!

The point of all this is that up to the age of 12 whilst the brainwaves operate in delta, theta and alpha, we are directly programmable. The child's brain at this stage can be likened to a computer that has no virus protection, there are no filters to help them discern what should or should not go in so everything, and I really do mean everything goes directly in. As multi-sensory beings, unlike adults who are only sensory beings (as in operating out of the five senses) a child operates beyond these senses.

The programmes that we develop during these formative years live on within us for a lifetime unless we become conscious of them. These programmes are what we have commonly come to know as beliefs and values. Whilst we know these are important the extent to which they drive us is desperately unappreciated.

Working with groups of leaders, one of my first requests of them is to write down their top ten values. So take a moment now to write down yours. If you think of more than ten, great, prioritise your top ten.

If you struggle to think of ten, you are amongst a mass population who consciously find it difficult to articulate their values. The same exercise is then requested but this time focused on beliefs. Quite often I get the question, are they not one and the same? The answer is yes and no!!

Values are the things that we hold dear in our lives such as family, love, friendships, hard work, ethics, religion, success, wealth, health, lifestyle etc. They guide how you live your life, how you orientate yourself to the world, how you prioritise the importance of the activities. For example one of my clients said that their number one priority was their family. A few days later this value was challenged to the ultimate test. Their work required their presence whilst their child was playing a part in his first nativity play. Given the client's number one priority was family you would think that they would have chosen to be with their child, however, no so, they chose their work, believing they had no other choice. So was family really their number one priority?

Beliefs on the other hand form the underlying structure for all the judgements and decisions we make and can include examples such as: I believe in good and evil; I believe that hard work is the key to success; I believe in God; I believe that beautiful people get the best deal; I believe in the sanctity of marriage; I believe in the inherent goodness of all humanity; I believe in an eye for an eye and a tooth for a tooth; I believe everyone has the resources they need to be whatever they want to be etc etc.

Each of these values and beliefs shape how we perceive the world and become our reality. So if I believe I am helpless then I will behave helpless and see the world as the cause of my helplessness. If I believe I can be whatever I want to be, it is likely I will be just that and I will see examples of others doing and being that.

Tom's conditioning developed his value that family come first, yet went against the grain of his belief that he could work and earn his own money. At the time, his value won precedent.

We've built an entire nation on values and beliefs that have been handed down through generation after generation. Tom happened to be born into an environment whose history had taught them to believe that men don't work and valued going with the majority rather than being individual. A rather powerful combination that held Tom prisoner.

The underlying structure is too powerful unless you know!

So how do you change this? How do you realise the beliefs and values you carry and the impact and effect they have on your life? These are million dollar questions. The simplest answer I can offer is self-awareness.

Many of us live life as an existence. We're not really present, in the moment. We rarely offer ourselves the opportunity to just stop, reflect, observe ourselves, to feel what's happening for us right now. We expend vast amounts of energy being either in the past or the future, thinking about later today, the next meeting, the holiday that's coming up, the night out that the weekend will bring, or yesterday when I did that, or when he/she said that to me, when I had that, when I went there. How many times a day do you stop to just experience the moment to know how you really feel?

In Action

A client sat in front of me recently and said: "I live in my head and don't know how to live any other way and I'm beginning to realise actually it is not that good for me to be living this way, I'm missing so much – I think?" We explored what he thought he was missing because by virtue of his statement something must have changed within him to allow him to know he was living in his head and that another option was possible. His three year old son had begun to interact with him much more having learned how to talk and walk. When he was with him he realised he behaved and thought differently and had started to access other parts of himself and found that he was having such fun, he'd laugh, cry and mimic his son's moods and playfulness. In doing so he'd discovered the depth of feeling and emotion that existed within him and started to think that perhaps this could be replicated in other parts of his life to enhance it.

I asked him if he ever just stopped for just a moment to be, so he could truly experience a moment/this moment. He said of course he did, when he was running he'd think a lot about where he is in life and plan what he was going to do with it and how. Once he said this he stopped and after a moment of reflection he said: "That's it! That's the difference I just told you what I do in my head and that's not what being is, so really the rare time that I am just being is when I'm with my son."

With further exploration my client realised that when he allowed himself he knew when he wasn't being true to himself but he had squashed this for so many years believing that it wasn't good to feel and that feelings served only to muddy waters, confuse things. He'd become the master of logic and objectivity and in the process forgotten how to access and flow with his own personal beliefs and values. Or was it that his belief was that logic prevails above all?

Everything Good is Outside – Giving power away
(most are at the mercy of apparent experts)

Robert Holden, founder of the Happiness Project and author of Be Happy coined the phrase, *Everything Good is Outside (EGO)*. We'll talk more about ego later but for now, Robert's analogy is crucial.

When we believe that everything good is outside, what we effectively do is offer our power out to others, believing that they have greater expertise than ourselves to manage our lives.

Perpetually in our lives we do this in ways that we are not even conscious of; my boss tells me what I should do; my wife tells me when and where to be; the media dictates what the latest fashion is and what's acceptable to wear; the beauty industry decides what beauty looks like; we watch an advert and decide yes, that's the product I need and when I have it then I'll be happy. When I have that car, I'll be happy. When I get that promotion then I'll be successful. When I live in that bigger house I'll have the space I need to have that family I want.

All of these things that we strive for and neither good nor bad, but they are all outside of us, we give ourselves and our power to them in the vain hope that they will make the difference we've been looking for.

Another example of giving power away is when you go to the doctor with an ailment. You believe that the doctor has the expertise to diagnose you, determine what you should do and you follow that advice without question. After all, the doctor is the expert right?

But the doctor only has a snippet of information and so is not diagnosing you, he is diagnosing your condition. There is little understanding of the underlying cause of your condition. Your symptoms are what your doctor is treating. So if you return again in two weeks time with a different ailment, he will prescribe a different treatment because again he is treating your condition – NOT YOU.

But you believe that he is the expert so perpetually you follow the advice given and ignore what your own body is telling you, what your gut instincts are screaming and what inherently you know, if you bother to check in with yourself. The doctor's job is not to diagnose you. Their training is in illness, not in people. They are trained to spot symptoms and treat the symptoms.

The same goes for voting in an election. Once I've ticked a box and then the whole country has ticked a box, we hand over to the Government to manage our economy, our society, our livelihood. We hand our power over to people who we trust will take responsibility for our country. But then we complain when they make decisions that we don't agree with, and worse, we stand by and resign ourselves to it being that way.

I often hear leaders complain about the things that affect their ability to perform. It's the economic downturn, the policy of Government, the staff don't know what they are doing, the structure isn't right etc. On and on the reasons for their performance are channelled outside of them. Yet when they, and their organisation are performing well, the reasons cited are: I worked hard, I kept focused, I was innovative.

When we operate on the belief that Everything Good is Outside we move consistently to blame everything else for our lacking. We are unable to be Response Able, and we lack the resource to take Response Ability. Sure we may not have direct control over economic circumstance or Government Policy, but we can make decisions about how we respond rather than react to it. Knowing this has a monumental impact on our lives as a number of leaders who kindly took part in interviews in research for this book have testified:

"I recognise that I always have choice about how I behave and respond in situations"

Jennifer Flint *Head of Organisation Development Isos Group*

"I don't think I can change..., but I can certainly change how I respond and deal with things and where I go"

Julie Kelly *Assistant Chief Executive Gentoo Group*

Cause is the reason but how do Humans reason
(society drives reasoning conditions)

When Everything Good is Outside we are never the cause, we are at effect of everything that is outside. And when we are not the cause, then we have no power to control what happens and everything happens TO us. This is a life filled with anxiety, tension, stress, dis-stress and dis-ease. The statistics speak for themselves and demonstrate this aptly.

Reflection Time

In 2008/09 an estimated 415,000 individuals in Britain, who worked in that year, believed that they were experiencing work-related stress at a level that was making them ill (prevalence), according to the Labour Force Survey (LFS).

Estimates from the LFS indicated that self-reported work-related stress, depression or anxiety accounted for an estimated 11.4 million lost working days in Britain in 2008/09. Hence the average days lost per case for stress, depression or anxiety, was 27.5 days.

The 2009 Psychosocial Working Conditions (PWC) survey indicated that around 16.7% of all working individuals thought their job was very or extremely stressful.

Coronary heart disease is the UK's biggest killer, with one in every four men and one in every six women dying from the disease. In the UK, approximately 300,000 people have a heart attack each year. Angina affects about one in 50 people, and in the UK there are an estimated 1.2 million people with the condition. (NHS, 2008)

According to the NHS also in 2008, almost a quarter of adults (24% of men and 25% of women aged 16 or over) in England were classified as obese.

In 2009, there was an average of 271 prescription items prescribed for alcohol dependency in England per 100,000 of the population. And in 2008, there were 6,769 deaths directly related to alcohol. An increase of 24% from 2001. Of these alcohol related deaths, the majority (4,400) died from alcoholic liver disease. (NHS)

During 2008/09, the NHS reported there were 207,580 people in contact with structured drug treatment services (those aged 18 and over). This is a 10.4% increase from the 2007/08 figures, where the number was 187,978. A larger number of men accessed treatment services than women (151,064 men compared to 56,516 women aged 18 or over).

This is indicative of the state of the health of those living at effect of the causes outside their control. Sadly it is also a general indictment of the health of the people of the UK, and therefore of the state of our country. We are self-evidencing the giving of our power.

Need

But what makes us consciously or unconsciously give our power away?

Earlier I said that every child is born with capacity for empathy. This is because as humans we are connected to one another in a way that offers us nurturing and sustenance we need to live (not exist). I also said that the average person relies upon another for love and support. Furthermore I said no man is an island and as humans we do not thrive when isolated from others.

This leads us to the belief that we need to be needed in order not to become separate or isolated. The extent to which we fear isolation determines our neediness and therefore how much self-power we believe we have, or we choose to give away.

Need is a condition/situation in which something is required or wanted. By virtue of this statement it implies that this can only be fulfilled externally by another person! And the result is that we become either needy or needed.

Need is also an emotional state of 'something's missing' e.g. the absence of another which equates to the absence of love. We use 'substitutes' to fill the gap yet somehow this doesn't fulfil us and we are left further bereft and wanting.

"something's missing"

We create Dependency so easily and without consciousness

It is therefore easy to see how dependency emerges, permeates, and becomes the driver for individuals. The result is conformity, the eagerness to fit and to belong and the compromise to ensure that we do.

The result is a judgemental society that by implication creates a herd mentality and a willingness to give personal power away.

Within this judgement we see ourselves as Superior to one and Inferior to another. A perfect example of this was the *Two Ronnies* and *John Cleese* sketch: *I Know My Place.* Whilst we all laughed at it and even today 40+ years after its first airing it still has a resonance that is inescapable.

The net result is that paradoxically we are both needy and needed and our society, culture and environment perpetuate this daily – unconsciously!! The impact of this is the development of generation after generation of humans who are becoming increasingly lost and unresourceful.

Unresourcefulness emerges when we don't use our competence or skill because we don't trust it and it may differentiate us or make us stand out from the crowd, which may isolate us. In not using it, we eventually forget we've got it.

In the need to avoid isolation or separateness we stay safe, ride with the tide around us and so we may never discover the innate competence, talents and abilities we have. When we're safe, or as some people have come to know it 'in our comfort zone', we never test or tap deep within, so we retain unfulfilled potential.

You only have to consider that some eight year olds who already consider themselves to be overweight, ugly, unworthy and unacceptable. What hope is there for the future if this is what we are creating?

We all suffer FEAR yet some use it to drive them whilst others use it to stifle – the net result is they offer their power to another in the hope that it will save them and keep them connected.

How we manifest Dependency is the key to unlocking it

In playing safe and small we become needy and in neediness we are never required to learn the art of responsibility because there are never any consequences. Someone else will always pick up the pieces. Think about the child who was over-nurtured, wrapped in cotton wool, got to adulthood and either never left the parental home or did and married a person disguised as his/her parent.

In Action

In my work I have come across many examples of this in practice. The first was a family consisting of mother, father and four boys. The boys are now in their late forties and fifties. Mother was extremely nurturing in her being and has always lavished love physically and practically on her children. Father was detached and distant concentrating his efforts on earning a living to keep his family. All four boys eventually left their mother, however, since their birth the family home has only once for one year not had one of them live with their parents.

21

The two eldest returned home in their late 40s and the eldest has never worked since returning and is now so obese he dares not leave the home. His mother is killing him with kindness!! The third married a carbon copy of his mother. The youngest one leads an independent life in which he connects on a surface level with others but protects his deep interior for fear of rejection, so has self-isolated from the loving connection of others.

Think also of the child who was consistently criticised or rejected to the extent they rebelled and went off the rails where the 'system' (prison/institute etc...) picked them up and took charge.

In Action

I have the privilege of being a Governor at an EBSD school (Emotional, Behavioural and Social Difficulties). The pupils in the school range from the age of 6 through to 16. The school is over-extended due to the level of demand for its unique and special services and its success in facilitating the transformation of these issues to enable the emergence of rounded adults who have found a way of accepting themselves without the overwhelming need for affirmation and attention from another.

In both these instances, the individual is moved to 'substitute' the parental role elsewhere. In the first instance never moving away from the parent or substituting the parent with a spouse/partner. In the second instance the child substitutes the parent for a teacher.

Another alternative includes substituting a boss for a parent. However it manifests we become passive in our life, seeking others to make decisions for us, to take control, to direct and guide us, to offer us validation, to stroke us when we're down, to give us momentum, to tell us what to do and when to do it, to govern our behaviour, to tell us how to think.

On the reversal alternatives include becoming a boss, a carer. And again, however this manifests we become the aggressor seeking to make decisions for others, to take control of them and for them, to direct and guide them, to validate and affirm them, to be the one that they always come to when they are down, to be their motivator, to tell/advise them what to do and when to do it, to govern and discern their behaviour judging it either good or bad and to direct their thinking.

In doing this we either avoid responsibility or become responsible for everything/everyone outside us. Either way we are not taking self-Response Ability.

In this fear of isolation and separateness we develop need, or more accurately the need to be needed. And as we can see, some of us become needy (dependent) and some of us become needed (dependable).

In his book '*The Art of Loving*,' Eric Fromm takes this theme to the extreme using the terms masochistic to describe the traits of the individual who is needy and sadist to describe the person who dominates the needy.

Both of these have negative connotations and it is in this depth that this book aims to explore how this has become the issue that has led to our nation and indeed the world becoming distressed, at war, deficient, reliant, dependent and generally no longer in possession of self-power or empowerment.

On a more positive note, need can also be a beautiful, nurturing and empowering way of living and being when it is born from a place of self-responsibility. This too will be explored throughout the following chapters.

Effect – we have the power to bring about the cause
(but the ownership of this we've given away
to so-called experts)

So if you're asking the question how do we overcome this and is it possible? The answer is an absolute and overwhelming YES, when we recognise it, become aware of it and develop, then take our innate capacity to be Response Able. We take and accept responsibility for self. We own our own life and the choices we make within it.

And the wonderfully good news is we only need to do this for self in order for it to affect others. Because as we role-model it we give others permission to unconsciously follow our lead. This is the true essence of a social leader and we are all social leaders! It really is that easy.

It is on the premise of dependency that the third sector has become so huge, not just in the UK but right the way around the world. The difficulty in this sector is that whilst the intentions are honourable to serve a cause, client, the underprivileged or to help someone in need, it is perpetuating its own need to be needed by the people it serves!!

"In the UK there is too much emphasis on paternalism and in the long run doesn't help, it makes people reliant and that's not helpful. But we all need a helping hand every now and again, and it is ok to lean occasionally but it shouldn't be an end game."

Julie Kelly *Assistant Chief Executive Gentoo Group*

Précis

Dependency: Contrary to self-belief that we are independent; dependency on others and their actions are such requirements, which determine all of our eventualities

Cause: "Whether you think you can or you can't, you are usually right." (Henry Ford) Our beliefs and values are self-determining.

Need: As individuals we are all, to some degree, needy or needed; therefore the very essence of dependency is derived.

Effect: Recognition of awareness leads to responsibility to ourselves and to others.

Dependency

CHAPTER TWO

Welfare - State

Any State is Temporal!

Where did the term State come from and what makes a state? The power of our language can be hugely underestimated. We use it so unconsciously without consideration for the depth of what we are saying. The profoundness of meaning can get lost, as we've already seen when looking at the deconstruction of dependency.

The incredibly interesting thing about **state** is the duality of the word itself:

As a noun (a content word that can be used to refer to a person, place, thing, quality, or action), the definition of **state** is a condition or mode of being; or being in a stage or form. This would suggest some form of movement and therefore a temporal or transient rather than permanent nature. From moment to moment we change our state depending on what we are thinking or how we are responding to external or internal stimuli.

As an adjective (a word that expresses an attribute of something) being 'in a state of' the adjective defines **state** of or relating to a body politic or as a territory occupied by a constituent administration. This completely changes the meaning of state and suggests some permanence or at least less transient and more medium to long term.

The polarity between the two is striking; one of transience and another of a longer-term nature; ownership supposes the noun belongs to the person whereas the adjective belonging to that which is outside.

Responsibility therefore shifts entirely when we use the word as an adjective rather than a noun and this is the source of the issues that the 'welfare **state**' is experiencing. By definition of the more permanent nature of the adjective we can devoid ourselves of responsibility and pass it over to the **state** to look after us. Recall also that dependency is a 'state' of relying or being controlled. We can also consider this to be more permanent or transient and how we choose to view it will determine the results we get.

After all we've demonstrated a level of permanence by virtue of the fact that our 'state' has looked after us for generations so why or even how would we know any different!!

Yet we know that this is unsustainable and a perpetually disabling way to treat people. Whilst the state has undoubtedly evolved, with deficits awry we must now question whether it has evolved purposefully, with honourable intentions of enabling conditions and expectations to which every person, by virtue of his or her existence as a human being, is entitled.

Or has it evolved to serve the Government of each day to enable their power and dominion over people despite democracy?

Whatever our history or reason for arriving at this place in our evolution, now more than ever in the history of civilisation it is undeniably time to shift, time to evaluate, learn from the past, appreciate what we've done well and where we can without doubt transform.

Well-fare

To labour the importance and underlying profundity of the structure of our language let's have a look at Well-Fare.

The definition of well is; good; possibility; favourable; and affording benefit or advantage. We could of course argue each of these in the context of welfare as we know it.

Fare means; to go; journey; be in a state; the condition of things; or the price of a passage.

Consider for a moment, each of these definitions. What is the price of a passage? The phrase *"there's no such thing as a free lunch"* springs to mind!!

Yet again though, the use of language rather distorts the intention behind the statement. It seems to have originated out of a speech by Henry Wallace (US President 1941 – 45) in an article he wrote in which he suggested a post-WWII worldwide economic regime offering *"minimum standards of food, clothing and shelter"* for people throughout the world and offering the opinion that *"if we can afford tremendous sums of money to win the war, we can afford to invest whatever amount it takes to win the peace."*

But what do we mean now in terms of the price of a passage – is there a price to be paid for welfare?

Consider now the definitions of fare in combination with the word 'well'. For example if you were 'good to go' or you could 'journey favourably' or 'be in a state of possibility'? When I put these meanings together in this way does your mind automatically conjure up and aptly describe our welfare state?

Welfare – health, happiness & good fortune (*has our State brought us this?*). When you combine both words as described we can experience the affirming nature and intention of welfare. But is that the definition?

In accordance with the Collaborative International Dictionary of English (v.0.48) the definition of welfare as a noun is; *"well-doing or well-being in any respect; the enjoyment of health and the common blessings of life; exemption from any evil or calamity; prosperity; happiness"*. I ask, is this what welfare is doing in the context of a welfare state?

In the same dictionary, WordNet, provide a definition of welfare as a noun *"governmental provision of economic assistance to persons in need"*. A rather different offering and again a polarity meaning.

I'm taken a step further at this point to ask, who decides that a person is in need?

And before we finally leave the underlying structure of the language one final definition is of welfare work, which is defined as *"organised efforts by a community to improve socioeconomic conditions for the disadvantaged"*. Two questions arise for me here. Firstly, is our State (Government) a community and do we truly have communities any longer in this age of individualism? And secondly who is organising the efforts? Take a moment to consider how you would answer these questions.

Historical Origins of the UK Welfare State

Commonly we have been led to believe that the Welfare State arose from the Beveridge Report in 1942. However, the reality is that it began as far back as the late Victorian era with the desire to provide cheap housing for the poor, the best healthcare for all and pensions, which made satisfactory provision for a comfortable retirement.

He who holds the magic wand has the power . . .

It can be traced back even further to the sixteenth century with the advent of the Poor Law Act 1556. Under the reign of Queen Elizabeth I, it enacted procedures for collecting charitable alms from the wealthier people of the parish to help the poor organised by churchwardens. By 1597, parishes were able to levy a poor rate, and this paid for the building of the first poorhouses.

The updated Poor Law Acts of 1601 continued to determine treatment of the poor and appointed each parish as overseers of the poor, and to collect the poor rate from the wealthier inhabitants. The 'parish' was understood to mean a place maintaining its own poor. Arising from the Act, legal action was available to remove those poor settled in another parish through formal process. Relief (or as we know it now, benefit) was only a right in the place of origin or settlement and had to be proved.

Further authorities were given to parishes through The General Workhouse Act 1723 enabling them to build their own workhouse or join with other parishes to do so.

After a review of the systems of administration and inconsistencies found therein, an investigation into the levels of poor relief and how it was being spent, in 1834 The Amendment to the Poor Law Act was passed decreeing that outside contributions (relief external to workhouses) to the poor would be stopped within two years. The aim of this act was to weed out what was then judged as the 'undeserving poor'. Poverty was not seen as a social problem: destitution was felt to be the result of character weakness.

The choice for any 'able-bodied' person was a workhouse or basically starvation. In rare cases charitable contributions could be made upon examination and qualification on a subjective basis on their worthiness to receive. The workhouses were harsh and difficult environments which separated families completely. All children, women and men worked hard-labour to earn their bed and food. This was deliberately in order to discourage people from wanting help. The social stigma attached to being a 'workhouse pauper' was extreme to the extent that dwellers wore uniforms with a 'P' for pauper. There was little regard for issues such as physical/mental health, age, or loss of parents.

Reflection Time

Reinforcing this view Thomas Carlyle (essayist and historian) wrote in 1839

"The New Poor Law is an announcement ... that whosoever will not work ought not to live. Can the poor man that is willing to work always find work and live by his work?
A man willing but unable to find work is...
the saddest thing under the sun."

Does this echo some of the words we're hearing from current (2011) Government?

Whilst vigorously enforced in the south of England immediately it didn't reach the north for some years and when it did the Anti-Poor Law movement was formed. By 1837 there were riots in Bradford, Huddersfield and Dewsbury (1838), which ultimately led to outside relief and supplements to incomes continuing.

In the wake of a severe outbreak of cholera in 1848-1849, Henry Mayhew (1812 – 1887 Chronicler of Victorian Labourers and the Poor) began a series of investigative pieces on the skilled and unskilled people who worked in trade. He showed that destitution was because of inadequate wages, not laziness or weakness.

By this time the society at large were becoming more conscious of the poverty around them and reformers started to emerge who gathered Information along with Poor Law medical officers. This helped to improve standards in the workhouses and also led to the 1848 Public Health Act.

Whilst the Poor Law Commission wanted to retain indoor relief (workhouses) new systems allowed for adaptation to local circumstances in order to provide outdoor relief. The parish remained the centre for the collection of poor rates until 1865. Outdoor relief continued to be inadequate.

Between 1834 and 1897 a plethora of Acts were passed including; Vaccination Act 1840; Lunatics (Care and Treatment) Act and Regulation of Asylums Act 1842; Poor Law Administration Act 1847; Union Chargeability Act 1865; and Prevention of Cruelty to, and Protection of, Children Act 1889.

The Beveridge Report – was Germany its role-model?

During this time, much was happening in Europe. In Germany 1878, under Bismarck, a form of 'welfare state' had commenced and by the 1880s Germany had developed a system of accident, health and pension insurance. In 1907, William Beveridge visited Germany to investigate their system further. What he seemed to have left him with was an ease that there needed to be no conflict between state action and the free market and indeed that social policies could strengthen the market and make it more efficient than ever.

During World War I, rent control was established and the Local Government Housing sector was established. State intervention also occurred in the provision of retirement income by Acts of Parliament in 1908, 1925 and 1948.

The Government in the midst of World War II and in throes of desperation for the plight of its population in 1942 released the Beveridge Report. It was historical and has guided the UK's approach to welfare since. Beveridge offered the report based on three principles:

"The first principle is that any proposals for the future, while they should use the full experience gathered in the past, should not be restricted by consideration of sectional interests established in the obtaining of that experience. Now, when the war is abolishing landmarks of every kind, is the opportunity for using experience in a clear field. A revolutionary moment in the world's history is a time for revolutions, not for patching."

"The second principle is that organisation of social insurance should be treated as one part only of a comprehensive policy of social progress. Social insurance fully developed may provide income security; it is an attack upon Want. But Want is one only of five giants on the road of reconstruction and in some ways the easiest to attack. The others are Disease, Ignorance, Squalor and Idleness."

"The third principle is that social security must be achieved by co-operation between the State and the individual. The State should offer security for service and contribution. The State in organising security should not stifle incentive, opportunity, responsibility; in establishing a national minimum, it should leave room and encouragement for voluntary action by each individual to provide more than that minimum for himself and his family."

Intentions were always honourable – but from what stance?

I'm not sure about you but in my opinion these three principles do not appear to exist in today's welfare state.

Based on principle one, we seem to still be restricted by sectional interests, for example each individual charity/cause or social organisation has its own funding pot. Health has its own budget in the NHS and there is a separate contribution to that. Housing had until the recent budget a specific fund, schools have a separate fund, local authorities have a separate fund, regional development in most constituents in the UK have their own pot. So how are we to ever have an approach that looks at the whole system, or more importantly the person as one entity rather than each individual condition or set of circumstances the person may be experiencing.

And was it revolutionary really? If it was did it take the lessons of the past to thoroughly revolutionise its future? Did the country need a revolution in the midst of a world war or did it need an evolution? Did the revolution mean that it wasn't to continue to evolve?

Principle two, social insurance is no longer 'one part only'. It has become the one and only for many. I've met only a handful of people who have intentionally invested personally in their health. Most believe that it is the domain of the NHS and it has full responsibility for our health! Of those that have set aside or considered investing in their health predominately this has been as a result of receiving some form of private health insurance through their employment. Of any that do invest voluntarily in their health it is generally in insurance, insuring them against illness. Rare do I ever hear of many investing directly in their health, in maintaining or creating health.

In terms of principle three, "the State in organising security should not stifle incentive, opportunity, responsibility". What incentive is there to get a job when you can earn as much on benefit. What incentive is there to save for retirement, to invest in health or to take ownership of your own destiny?

In Action

"Congratulations Jack, just sign these forms here and you will never have to work another day in your life," the Consultant's face beaming with this news. Jack looked at him confused and bemused. The Consultant explained that if Jack set foot back in the baker's factory where he worked he would die because of an effect flour has on his lung condition so was offering him the opportunity to remain on disability benefit for the rest of his life. Jack was in his early thirties.

In disbelief and feeling that this was not cause for celebration he went home to share the news with his family, who cracked open the beer and welcomed Jack to his new life, the life that so many of his family, friends and neighbours shared. They talked to him of how much he could now join them at the 'club', have lay-ins every morning and never have to worry again about where the next penny was coming from.

Jack was appalled and as he watched his aunt hobble up to him with her walking stick, it suddenly occurred to him that she had never needed the stick yet now was fully dependent upon it (in her mind).

Jack fell into a deep depression at the thought of being so valueless to society. In the depths of his depression he had an epiphany when he realised his managerial skills could be utilised in another food environment. He sought another job in a food factory and one day realised his skills were as a manager and in fact these could be used in any environment. The doors of possibility and opportunity opened to him in that moment and today he works in the social sector helping people to help themselves resolve neighbourhood disputes.

Jack was a rarity in his community who at large had become stifled of incentive, opportunity and responsibility, ingrained now in their belief that they were entitled to be 'looked after'. Despite being ostracised by them Jack had taken responsibility for his own life, his belief was that there was no point in living if he could not contribute.

There are thousands, and perhaps even more of Jack in this country but there are many, many more like those in his community who have become not only stifled but completely disabled of self-responsibility.

This was not how it was intended to be. Daily we pay the price for creating such a dependent state. In the UK Public Expenditure is approximately 45% of GDP or about £600 billion of spend. Of the total spend, around 52% is spent on welfare, pension and health (2010).

Financially the figures just don't stack up and clearly we cannot afford to continue in this way. David Cameron (Prime Minster 2010) himself contests to this:

Reflection Time

"£1 in every £3 is spent on welfare. You have to deal with the extent of welfare dependency in this country if you're going to get the budget deficit under control and if you're going to have a system that encourages work."

Even more importantly though we cannot afford to continue to perpetuate the level of human detriment, powerlessness and therefore welfare issues, which again David Cameron recognises:

Reflection Time

"….the case of a single mum earning a few hundred pounds a week, and if she tried to work more 96 pence in every pound was taken away from her. That's wrong, that's outrageous… we all know cases at the moment where you know you meet someone who's desperate to work, but if they work they lose their housing benefit…"

As these statements from David Cameron testify, never before in history has Government been so open, approachable and actively seeking our voice on perspectives, ideas and ways to truly empower the people of the UK.

Will Smith (actor) once said: *"Greatness lives on the edge of destruction."* We've done the destruction so now's the time to step into our greatness. Now is the time to step away from judgment, superiority and entitlement and step toward the fullness of our self-responsibility as beings.

As a democracy we elect Government to lead us. This does not mean that we also need to give over our personal power and responsibility for ourselves, which is effectively what we have done. It is time to take self-responsibility for creating the life we really want to live.

It is time to be brave, confront our fears, truly evaluate our values and beliefs. Stop focusing on the financial means and use the resources already there inherent in the people.

It is time for a new education, a new way of seeing our world, a new way of encouraging and enabling contribution from all to ensure the people have a purpose for being rather than an entitlement to exist.

But who's going to facilitate this change? Simply those already equipped and they are the country's leaders of organisations with a direct (and indirect) social purpose; the leaders who believe in the capacity of mankind to manage self who in authenticity seek for the greater good of human wellbeing; the ones who help people help themselves; the ones who possess a genuine desire and ability to facilitate and innovate with the people to create sustainable, self-empowered solutions to the issues we face. These are the leaders who know that if one goes down we all go down.

But how?

The How question impedes, it is overwhelming as it requests detailed data and information. We could spend years collecting, analysing, cataloguing, evaluating and judging but all of it *for what purpose?*

So perhaps a more appropriate starting point would be to ask:

What does it look/sound/feel like when we have achieved a society of people who have capacity for self-ownership, self-responsibility and are self-sustaining?

On a purely practical level we have a multitude of agencies fighting against one another unconsciously for their cause. Each cause is only one facet of the human; a condition e.g. poverty, cancer, dementia, worklessness, homelessness etc...

We need to pull together to galvanise our combined resources and expertise, and get focused on wholeness of a person and the overall outcome each of us in our own individual way is attempting to achieve for society.

The answer offered by the UK Government in 2010 is the 'Big Society'. Whilst the principle to devolve power to families, neighbourhoods, communities, and the voluntary sector is noble, it does not go far enough yet!

Bar an already established agency, 'The Compact', set up in 2007 under the Office of the Third Sector, which is a national agreement between the Government and the voluntary and community sector on how relations between the two should be conducted, the 'Big Society' has not considered the way in which it will bring together businesses or third sector organisations to serve the nation as a whole.

Nor does it outline the structural change that is required in our economy to support at the very least one basic capacity issue, the issue of time for people to fully engage.

Furthermore it has not considered or articulated the meaning of shared responsibility, for example through disparate or even opposing income groups, never mind geographic, political or cultural differences.

At present our £35bn voluntary sector is 40% sustained by state support. And despite the Government's promise to support the sector to enable the 'Big Society', the new Office for Civil Society (which replaced Labour's Office of the Third Sector) has already cut £11m from organisations that support volunteering (2010).

So the dependency continues and we continue to condone it!!

Précis

State: is only a temporal condition.

Welfare: (Well-Fare) are we 'good to go' and 'journeying favourably' or are we offering welfare as a "governmental provision of economic assistance to persons in need" with the long-term effect of creating deeper dependency.

Ownership: Incentive to take responsibility and explore all opportunities.

How to deliver welfare: To combine all our resources and expertise.

CHAPTER THREE

The Social/Third Sector

Let's take something simple and make it complex!!!

The sector has many different guises and depending on your perception can have not only many different connotations, but actually many different names:

- The Third Sector
  (sometimes described as the Tertiary Sector)
- The Civic Sector
- The Voluntary (Community) Sector
- The Social Enterprise Sector
- The Social Sector

The result of such diverse terminology is confusion. The meaning and activities contained mean different things to different people and are all further dependent upon the connection to, or point entry for the individual. The community, voluntary, and not-for-profit sectors are frequently taken to consist of the 'Third Sector', yet each of these sectors or sub-sectors are quite unique in character.

Third Sector (Tertiary Sector)

The Third Sector is defined as voluntary or non-profit sector of an economy. Described as *"an intermediary space between business and government where private energy can be deployed for public good"* by Jim Joseph (President, Council On Foundations).

Previous to the UK's current coalition Government the department set up to assist the sector was 'The Office of the Third Sector'. Here the 'Third Sector' was also defined as *"the place between State and (the) private sector".*

The Third Sector includes an incredibly diverse scope and type of organisation:

- **Non-governmental organisations**
- **Voluntary organisations**
- **Community groups**
- **Tenants and residents groups**
- **Faith groups**
- **Housing Associations/Registered Social Landlords**
- **Most co-operatives and social enterprises (provided profits are retained for the benefit of the members or community served)**
- **Most sports organisations**
- **Grant making trusts**
- **Private clubs**

However, conversely The Tertiary Sector is described as *'administrative and service sector of the economy'* and provides services to the general population and businesses. Activities associated with this sector include retail and wholesale sales, transportation and distribution, entertainment, restaurants, clerical services, media, tourism, insurance, banking, healthcare, and law. The fine line between the Tertiary and the Third sector seems to be profit or non-profit or to be more precise a commercial activity versus a social activity.

As mentioned 'The Office of the Third Sector' has been afforded a new identity. And interestingly the department has now been renamed 'The Office for Civil Society', which is defined as supporting Voluntary and Community Groups and Social Enterprises.

The Civic Sector

Why have the UK Government changed to 'The Office of Civil Society' and what does the change mean or at least where is it intended to direct the UK? Perhaps it is intended to support its 'Big Society' proposals?

Michael Edwards (author of Civil Society) has proposed three dimensions to the term *Civil* Society – as associational life, as the good society and as arenas for public deliberation. He believes that it takes the combination of all three to make an effective, intentional and inclusive outcome.

We learn in many different environments, places, and ways and this learning creates our values and beliefs. In order to become a *Civil* Society there must be some semblance of commonality in our values and beliefs and we need to recognise that voluntary/not-for-profit are by no means the only sources, hence acknowledging and embracing an associational life.

The good society goals are based on the trueness of equality which is the aim of voluntary/not-for-profit organisations. The success in achieving good society goals according to Edwards *"has always been based on social contracts negotiated between government, business and citizens."*

And finally 'arenas for public deliberation' is the concept of freedom of speech and public voice ensuring the capacity to develop shared interests and to see oneself as connected in difference and sameness.

What Edwards is keen to express is the level of ambiguity in the terminology of the 'Civil Society' and the dangers and threats this poses to creating a harmonised society.

It seems that despite the change in focus the difficulties faced through our current terminologies of 'Third Sector' continue to be perpetuated by the 'Civil Society'.

Our circumstances call for our leaders to provide clarity not further ambiguity!

The Voluntary (Community) Sector

The term 'voluntary organisation' covers a wide variety of non-profit entities and is considered to engage staff (on a paid basis) working for a social or community purpose. Generally these organisations are constituted and therefore formal.

In contrast the community sector comprises of organisations active on a local or community level usually funded and dependent upon voluntary rather than paid effort. Generally they are informal in their establishment.

The two therefore may seem mutually exclusive yet as this description demonstrates, are in fact co-dependent. In the main this sector relies upon both public and private funding to service and facilitate its operations.

The fundamental of this sector being it operates for the benefit of society or has a 'social purpose'.

This suggests that organisations within this sector arise from direct community benefit motives. Yet the not-for-personal-profit sector is also considered to include other types of organisations (such as co-operatives and mutuals) and more recently Governmental institutions (such as Housing Associations/ Registered Social Landlords) that have been spun off from Government, although still operating fundamentally as a social purpose entity. These entities may, by some, be considered to be quasi-private or quasi-public sector.

Further confusion in definition!

The Voluntary and Community Action for London organisation offers an alternative approach to provide clarity by defining the sector as tiered:

1. First-tier organisations are those working directly with people on a defined activity to meet charitable objectives, e.g. womens' refuges, training projects, cancer care. They may also be referred to as client delivery, grass roots, street level etc.

2. Second-tier organisations are those working directly with other Voluntary and Community Sector organisations to meet charitable objectives, e.g. councils for voluntary service, Advice UK. They can be generalist or specialist and may be referred to as providing business-to-business support, infrastructure or co-ordinating organisations.

3. Third-tier organisations primarily support second-tier organisations.

The Social Enterprise Sector

According to the UK Government's definition, the social enterprise sector includes organisations which *"are businesses with primarily social objectives whose surpluses are principally reinvested for that purpose in the business or in the community, rather than being driven by the need to maximise profit for shareholders and owners".* Examples include co-operatives, building societies, development trusts and credit unions.

As the term 'enterprise' may imply these organisations operate a purposeful or industrious undertaking, or a business venture. Whilst the voluntary and community sector relies mainly on funding, social enterprises are predmoninantly self-funded through trading products and services.

The Social Sector/Economy

Based on all of the varying definitions and activities of this sector, we can see that the social economy spans economic activity in the community, voluntary and social enterprise sectors. The economic activity, as with any other economic sector, includes: employment; financial transactions; the occupation of property; pensions; trading, etc. In fact this sector employs three quarters of a million people in the UK (2010) and rising. That's nearly 20% of the population!

Ultimately irrespective of whether the organisation is informally organised or formally constituted, the entity is therefore by its nature an organisation. And basically, an organisation in its simplest form (and not necessarily a legal entity, e.g, corporation or LLC) is a person or group of people intentionally organised to accomplish an overall, common goal or set of goals.

An organisation must have a leader who facilitates the establishment of the organisation's vision, mission, values, strategic aims and ensures that its systems and processes are aligned with achieving these.

It is to all intents and purposes a business in its broadest sense in that it is an economic system designed to exchange services (and goods) to its market for one another or for money. Many of the people I've worked with in this sector simply do not understand this element of their organisation's being.

Reflection Time

In conversation with the Chair of a Trust Specialist school recently I asked why they were seeking sponsorships and funding to pay for them to 'give away' their expertise. I was met with a rather blank face. The thought that they could charge for their expertise had never even occurred to them and was seen to be unethical and in some way an attack on their values and beliefs. The value of their expertise was to be seen by sponsors wishing to support it as a gift that should be shared rather than a competence that could be exchanged in return for other services or money.

The paradox of this of course is that they still have to 'sell' their expertise and the hard way to do that is to ask for sponsorship, donation and funding rather than offering it to those who need to know it would be useful in exchange for something else (be that money or their services).

This is a fundamental point within the sector that has the ultimate effect of perpetuating dependency by continuously gifting rather than seeking a mutual exchange, which has the effect of creating a mutual participation and therefore respect and value, which creates empowerment.

Ultimately for the purposes of this book and clarity of the wide range of ambiguities in definition within this sector I will from herein refer to the collective as 'The Social Sector' comprising a social economy. At the heart of this sector what we are truly seeking is health and happiness for all citizens.

The purpose of this sector is to facilitate resource to help people help themselves – not just to help and therefore do it for them!!

So why is this not our focus or is it or do we just
perceive it is when all we are really doing
is perpetuating dependency!!

I have asked many people this question so please take a moment to consider it for yourself.

Reflection Time

Do you know of any charity or voluntary organisation
that has resolved the cause it was set up to alleviate?

If you do I'd really like to hear from you because this is a rare find indeed! I hear you say that in the case of poverty or some diseases this is not possible. And indeed you could probably say the same for Peace! Jeremy Gilley (of Peace One Day) probably wouldn't agree. In response to my question what enables him to continuously influence so well even when he comes up against comments such as *"Yeah it's a nice idea mate but its really just symbolism,"* Jeremy simply said *"...because I believe change is possible, I believe peace is possible and its in that context that I do what I do..."*

Where there is a will there is a way...and our job as leaders in this sector is to seek out that way using all of the resources at our disposal and in particular the resource contained within those suffering the effects of whatever that 'cause' is. This is why Jeremy Gilley cites the women, children and men that he has met over the continents of the world as his driver:

"So that all stems from a lot of human beings that I've spoken to,
a lot of the women and children in desperate situations all over
the world who are really affectively, if you like, the foundation
for my thinking and for my passion and my enthusiasm and my
tenacity and my belief. They are me, we are the same thing."

Jeremy Gilley, Peace One Day

Invariably, however, we can become or play the role of **Saviours, Helpers, Activists, Champions, Advocates, Carers**, or **Heroes**. None of these roles lend themselves easily to empowering another to do it for themselves... they all inadvertently make the mistake of judging the person they act on behalf of as incapable of acting on their own behalf. In playing any of these roles, we rob another of the ability to be in their own power.

Is this a society that we want to live in? A society that is built on judgment, superiority, inequality, and those who can whilst others can't!! If it's possible for one man, surely it is possible for another. However, what makes it not possible is firstly the lack of belief in their ability; secondly the lack of support for them to bring forth their own ability; and thirdly their own belief in their lack of ability – perpetuated by the offer of help!

Co-dependency is toxic

We have come to distort our helping role in this sector and see it as a God-given sovereign that we are the only ones who can 'save' or 'rescue' these apparently needy people!!

Whilst we act in these roles we become dependent ourselves, needing to be needed by the 'needy', in order to fulfil what we believe to be a worthy cause, a personal mission, and dare I say it, for some a ticket into heaven!!

. . . Eventually the organisation becomes co-dependent on the client to remain operational. Funding streams become manipulated, services now lean towards funding requirement rather than the needs of those we serve, and our mission becomes about keeping the organisation in business rather than the purpose for which we established in the first instance.

We need to get back to the basics to stop the merry-go-round of dependency and co-dependency persisting. The impetus must always be on empowering the individual, group or community we are there to service and never anything else, no matter what the economic or environmental conditions.

There is still only one pot of money in the world … do we carry on fighting for our share!

Money makes the world go around, or so the saying goes. Like it or not it is the currency most recognised and in order to facilitate the work we do in the social sector we need currency. However we look at it, the social sector DEPENDS on others for money, whether we are actively making it (as in social enterprise) or actively taking it (receipt of funding, sponsorship, legacies or donations).

Each social organisation is out there actively seeking finances to support its endeavours. Each in its own unique way, with its cause, its passion, or its mission. Each appealing to an audience, some the same and some different. Each focused on attaining what it needs to eradicate, raise awareness, find the cure, develop communities, breathe new life into deprived or run down areas, educate, care for and so much more. Yet what we fail to see is that actually in this approach all we end up doing is fighting against one another for a share for our cause. And whilst each cause has without doubt got people at its heart, each cause is a 'part' of the person, a 'part' of society, a 'part' of a bigger picture.

It is time to join forces, not least for the combined and synergistic benefits this offers in terms of differing perspectives, knowledge, competence, and other resource. Not least just for the financial benefits. Most of all it is time to join forces for our common desire to enable the wholeness of a person, of a people, and of a society.

When we focus only on one condition, one cause, one fight, we lose sight of context and get blind-sided. We can't see the wood for the trees any longer or the light that exists between the trees, only the obstacles of one tree after another.

Reflection Time

"The most valuable 'currency' of any organisation is the initiative and creativity of its members. Every leader has the solemn moral responsibility to develop these to the maximum in all his people. This is the leader's highest priority."

W. Edwards Deming in Principle Centred Leadership

The issues in society are now beyond money

The issues our society faces are beyond money, and not to disregard the importance of economic prosperity, money is not the route to happiness or the only route to empowerment.

In Action

I served on the board of a youth initiative. Our initiative manager was on the phone to a funding provider one day, explaining the depth of deprivation that existed in the area we worked and how the initiative was helping youths who otherwise would not have attained a standard of education comparable with their peers in a private estate, and who, through the initiative were reducing the levels of ASBOs, teenage pregnancies etc. whilst increasing aspirations. When she came off the phone a young boy approached her, having overheard her conversation and asked if he was deprived.

This youth did not see himself as deprived. He did not live in a bubble unaware of the fact that others led different, or perhaps more prosperous lives than him. He was happy. He had family around him, a tight-knit community of support, some great friends that he met both at the initiative and outside of it, schooling that he enjoyed and a life generally that he considered to be good for him.

Money was not his driver and he did not feel that he was lacking it in anyway. However, somewhere a statistic for the area he lived in, determined it to be included in the Index of Deprivation and therefore allocated as an area that required additional support. Hence the youth initiative was set up as part of the community plan by the Housing Association that owned the estate.

This story is not told to take away from the amazing work that the initiative is doing and the wonderful results it has and continues to yield. It is merely a demonstration that money is only ONE driver, not THE driver. Ultimately the community does much to keep the initiative open and support its activities and without their part, it would not still be in existence – even with its funding!

We need to see the world anew
If we always do what we have always done,
We will always get what we have always got

At the risk of repeating myself, which I will continue to do throughout this book to drive home the importance of what I'm saying, at the heart of the social sector is the desire to create health and happiness for all citizens – Our Vision. The purpose therefore of this sector and Our Mission, is to facilitate resource to help people help themselves – not just to help and therefore do it for them!!

Repeating Henry Ford's quote: *"If you think you can or you think you can't, you are probably right."* I was introduced to this quote when I was in my teens. It was a throwaway remark from a boss who offered no explanation. I guess she felt it was self-explanatory. Whilst I heard the words and they stuck with me it wasn't until my twenties that I was afforded the opportunity through adversity to test its message and then finally the penny dropped. We are what we believe!

If you believe it is about money, then it will be about money. But you must know that this poses a limitation, which you will reflect directly out to those you work with and on behalf of.

If you believe it is about inequality or disadvantage then it is. Know that this perpetuates inequality and disadvantage.

If you believe it is about a condition, a cause, a mission, then it will be just about that condition, cause or mission. And again know that in holding this belief, you limit the capacity of those you work with and on behalf of to recognise what's good in their life rather than what's not.

If you believe that those you work with and on behalf of are incapable in some way, then they will be incapable in some way. Yet again, know that you impose this limitation upon them, just like it could have been the result of the young boy in the youth initiative.

The Question we need to ask now is "Can we give/take other than of money to build and create a society in which health and happiness for all thrives?"

The answer is a resounding yes. We have at our disposal always a richness and abundance of resource (far more powerful than money). When we focus upon what health is rather than what illness is, when we focus upon what happiness is than what struggle is, when we focus on what we want rather than what we don't and finally when we focus on abundance rather than lack, the pathway to health, happiness and wellbeing illuminates in front of us.

We need to stop thinking of deficit, plugging gaps and short-termism strategy. We need to start thinking about holistic healing, the wider context of what the purpose of the social sector is and the bigger picture of a society filled with empowered citizens who take responsibility for self, take ownership for their own health, happiness and wellbeing and who value the contribution they make to society at large and to their own and others lives. We want sustainability not temporal solutions.

As a leader or contributor to the social sector in anyway NOW more than ever before, is your time. Your gift is to step up and into the fullness of what you do and who you are. Take the time to evaluate why you are in this sector. Consider the following questions:

Reflection Time

__What do you want__ in return for what you offer?

__What fulfilment do you get__ from doing what you do?

__What beliefs do you have__ that limit (unconsciously) those you are there to empower?

__How much of what you do__ has the pure aim of empowering others?

__Do you observe__ the greater society or just those in your area of expertise?

__Do you recognise__ the abundance of resource available at your fingertips?

__Do you recognise__ those that you work with and on behalf of as a resource in and of themselves?

__Do you see__ them as already having all the resources they need to fulfil their potential?

__Do you see__ you as already having all the resource you need to fulfil your own potential?

__Do you believe__ that the only limitation a human being meets is himself?

These questions are offered to enable you to assess your alignment with the social sector. I urge you please if you feel having answered these questions that this sector is not for you, please step out and go forward to do that which brings you alive. In the words of Howard Thurman: *"Don't ask what the world needs. Ask what makes you come alive, and go do it. Because what the world needs is people who have come alive."*

Take ownership for yourself. You cannot wait on others to provide, you are the creator. Collectively as servants to this sector, we are the creators. As a leader or contributor to the social sector you role-model the way for others, your influence **cannot not** be felt by everyone you touch and I know you want this to have a lasting positive effect. As Ghandhi reflected so beautifully simple: *"Be the change you wish to see."*

Become Conscious and Stop being the cause
Become the Effect & Enabler

Précis

The Social Sector: Includes any organisation that has been established to fulfil a social purpose to heal and enable society.

Mission: The sole purpose of these is to help people help themselves.

Vision: To create Health and Happiness for all citizens.

The Social/Third Sector

The Social Leader and Social Leadership

I've asked many a leader (social or otherwise) what their definition of leadership is and rare do I hear the same answer twice. However, there are themes within that are similar and these include the words such as; control; planning; organising; communication; value; respect; influencing; guiding; and role-modelling.

I'm continually fascinated by the diversity of the answers and can tell as soon as I enter an organisation the type of leadership style that exists. Undoubtedly this stems directly from the most senior (or strongest) person in the organisation, so I can pretty much guess the words they'll use to describe what leadership is to them.

Their leadership reverberates through the organisation and if you're paying attention you can see, hear and feel it all around you. It is in the literature, the brand, the structure, the processes and systems, the way in which the customer is perceived, the way of being of the staff, the culture, the way that stakeholders engage.

We Cannot Not In-Fluence

A Leader leads by example, whether intentional or not

To contextualise this chapter it would be useful at this time to reflect on some definitions, and interesting enough most dictionaries refer to leadership as controlling a group or as the function or role a leader holds.   Leadership is so much more and perhaps the following offerings of great writers (and leaders) can illuminate.

Peter Drucker: The forward to the Drucker Foundation's 'The Leader of the Future' sums up leadership : *"The only definition of a leader is someone who has followers."* To gain followers requires influence but doesn't exclude the lack of integrity in achieving this. Indeed, it can be argued that several of the world's greatest leaders have lacked integrity and have adopted values that would not be shared by many people today.

John C Maxwell : *"Leadership is influence – nothing more, nothing less."* (21 Irrefutable Laws of Leadership.) This removes position or title and opens doors to all. It widens the breadth of leadership beyond followers. There is a suggestion contained that puts integrity and trustworthiness at its heart, however, we all know that influence can be yielded through fear!!

Warren Bennis: *"Leadership is a function of knowing yourself, having a vision that is well communicated, building trust among colleagues, and taking effective action to realise your own leadership potential."* Bennis infers that leadership is innate within and accessed only when you are true to your own core and authentic in your being.

John Quincy Adams: *"If your actions inspire others to dream more, learn more, do more and become more, you are a leader."* Reinforcement that leadership is influence.

Oscar Wilde: *"Those who try to lead the people can only do so by following the mob."* This offering by Wilde confirms that leadership is not a role to be played it is a fundamental way of being (not doing). In 'trying' to do, authenticity is lost.

What these definitions offer in terms of leadership is the understanding that everyone is a leader in their own right. Everyone has capacity for leadership. Everyone has the right to lead their own life. Everyone consciously or not, leads others by their very being.

A person's capacity to recognise themselves as a leader is determined by their ability to look inward and connect with their own personal source.

"We carry within us the wonders
we seek without us."

Sir Thomas Browne

The social leader understands this but may not live it. The 'Authentic' social leader, however, differs.

Authentic Social Leaders

This quote by Northcutt holds the key to unleashing this difference

> *"The goal of many leaders is to get people to think more highly of the leader. The goal of a great leader is to help people to think more highly of themselves."*

J. Carla Northcutt:

Simply put authentic social leaders differ because they believe they were born to manifest the fullness of themselves in order to facilitate the manifestation of the greatness in others. One of the leaders I interviewed in research for this book, Cormac Russell (Nurture Development) said: *"...I believe that as leaders if you're going to enable people to look within, you need to do that for yourself."* What Cormac demonstrates is that the authentic social leader can facilitate so effectively because they have taken opportunity to truly engage with their purpose in life, they take ownership and responsibility for themselves first and foremost.

They see the lessons in everything and can easily turn their pain to gain. They permanently see the potential in all things, matter, nature, life and crises. Every challenge is an opportunity to learn and grow. In response to the question about the qualities of an authentic social leader another interviewee, Jeremy Gilley of Peace One Day said *"...a sense of not worrying about failing. Fail, go for the failure and first of all see the reality of the matter, no matter what anybody thinks. It doesn't matter what anyone thinks if you fail. If you trust your vision and it's true to you then go for it."*

The authentic social leader accepts responsibility for their influence in society and helps others to learn and progress. They take risks trusting their creativity. They make value-based as well as belief-based decisions. They consistently review both their values and beliefs to ensure they can continue to be served by them and therefore serve others in a manner that empowers.

Humility and humbleness only scratch the surface of how these leaders operate. Norman Vincent Peale describes it aptly with this quote: *"The more you lose yourself in something bigger than yourself, the more energy you will have."* These leaders do not even consider the concept of humble or humility. They do not live for personal recognition, they do not live for personal satisfaction. They live to inspire others to live.

The most appropriate explanation of humility applies *"humility is attentive patience"* (Simone Well). Authentic social leaders exercise attentiveness to all and in all they do. Their patience can be described as that of a Saint. More appropriately is their ability to persist with tenacity, with determination and resilience. They do not compromise but they will sacrifice for the greater good.

These leaders know that supporting is not always enabling. They do not look on another with pity or sympathy. They rarely have lived a life without challenge themselves and just as they know they learn from their life, they respect that others learn from theirs too and move only to facilitate their recognition of this. At times this leader may hold a space for a person who has fallen, and in it, will help them to accept where they are and bring forth their resource to allow them to move out and beyond. This is empathy. Empathy empowers, sympathy disables and these leaders know the difference.

Empathy is defined as the power of understanding and imaginatively entering into another person's feelings. Because these leaders act beyond multi-sensory perception they can access energetically the field of another. Compassion is probably a more appropriate way of describing this, which requires you share your passion with others. The passion of others in pain, in shock, in grief, in loss, in anger, in happiness, in joy. This leader knows these because he had the courage to never shy from truly experiencing his own. Compassion allows this leader to feel those difficult emotions and the pain that lies beneath them as well the fear that the joyous ones may only be fleeting and perhaps are undeserving!

Authentic social leaders believe in human capacity and an individual's ability to create their own destiny. They are themselves, therefore why could another human not be? This does not come from a position of believing that others should be like them, it comes from knowing that every individual has their own unique resources to live the life they believe to be right for them.

Above all the authentic social leader knows that their ticket to heaven is not in what they do, heaven is already here in who they are!

Being Audacious

I was recently invited to work with a social organisation to facilitate their leadership in the development of an Audacious Ambition. This was music to my ears. I set about preparing a presentation to the leadership on my interpretation of their requirements. As I did I started questioning the meaning of audacious, to me it meant innovatively ambitious, paving a new way, and stretching of everything they believed was possible. But I wanted to know what it meant to them!

As is my style and my passion for the energetic value of language I sought the definition. The first I found said 'fearlessly, often recklessly daring; bold'. This was not a reckless organisation, in fact in many ways my experience suggested it highly risk-adverse. It was not my role to judge this but to raise awareness.

Then I got to thinking about fearless. The organisation can only be fearless when its leaders are fearless, free from constraint, inhibition and judgement, able to be vulnerable, courageous and brave. I was excited to engage with this and saw it as a wonderful opportunity to facilitate their bringing this to bear in new ways on behalf of those it served.

The second definition I found was 'unrestrained by convention or propriety; insolent; spirited and original'. This resonated with my original interpretation.

Armed with this additional information I went back to preparing the presentation, yet I had been so struck by the scope and the depth of meaning of the word audacious, I scrapped everything I had originally designed and started afresh.

I looked inward and considered feedback outward. Throughout my life I have been accused of being audacious and I have also been admired for being audacious and I suddenly realised the polarity of this response to me. Some had seen my audaciousness as reckless, some as spirited and some in between.

I decided ultimately to design something that would allow them to experience audaciousness for themselves in its fullest scope. The feedback suggested that this indeed was a very brave strategy that in the immediate aftermath led them to reject working with me. However, upon reflection they realised what they had experienced and its purpose and decided they wanted more.

It is easy sometimes as a leader to allow ourselves to get in the way of the greater good of the organisation and therefore its purpose for being. But the strength inner knowingness prevails in the authentic social leader.

These leaders had found themselves most uncomfortable by what I had designed for them to experience. Their defences rose, their personal survival instinct jarred, their ego had led them to believe I had tested and judged them. Yet they had the strength to look within, reflect, evaluate and learn. This takes courage, compassion and dare I say it audaciousness!

This is the essence of authentic social leadership. As Stephen Covey says: *"As you live your values, your sense of identity, in-*

tegrity, control, and inner-directedness will infuse you with both exhilaration and peace. You will define yourself from within, rather than by people's opinions or by comparison to others. 'Wrong' and 'right' have little to do with being found out."

I had been neither right nor wrong in my strategy I had been guided from within. They had been neither right nor wrong in their response, they allowed themselves to be guided from within. In turn this allows them to take the organisation forth in audacious spirit to lead and role-model those they serve to be inspired in their own audaciousness.

As leaders in the social sector we need to be audacious in every sense. We need to be fearless to pave the way for others and show them fear is in the mind. We need to be bold and boldly go where no others have. And so at times we need to be recklessly daring to demonstrate that limitations are man-made.

A beautiful example of this in practice is an organisation called Peace One Day (POD), founded by an equally beautiful man called Jeremy Gilley. In 1999, preoccupied with questions about the fundamental nature of humanity and the most pressing issues of our time, Jeremy launched POD and set out to find a starting point for peace. He had a mission: to document his efforts to establish the first ever annual day of global ceasefire and non-violence with a fixed calendar date. A rather audacious ambition but one which he firmly believes is achievable. Initially he was met with cynicism and remarks such as, *"he is either mad or a genius"* or *"yeah it is a nice idea, but it's just symbolism."* In his interview with me he said: *"You've just got to be very true to what it is you want to achieve. I know what it is I want us to do and that's manifest a global cease fire and I'm now, irrespective of what anybody thinks, going to do my absolute best with the support, help and guidance of others, to nail it... because I believe change is possible and I believe Peace is possible."*

Because of this audaciousness, and Jeremy's authenticity and absolute belief, two years into his journey he achieved his primary objective when the 192 member states of the United Nations unanimously adopted 21 September as an annual day of global ceasefire and non-violence on the UN International Day of Peace. But his work continued and continues today true to his original mission POD looks to engage all sectors of society, including governments, organisations of the United Nations system, regional and non-governmental organisations and individuals in observance of 21 September, through the practical manifestation of non-violence and ceasefire in accordance with UN GA Resolution 55/282, and encourage action on Peace Day that creates a united and sustainable world.

In this sector more than any, we need to be unrestrained by convention or propriety. Convention and propriety arise from judgement, our sector has the responsibility of seeing the world anew because following the pack leaves us in no better a position than we are today. We are the spirited ones that are abundant in energy and originality of thinking and being. As Steve Jobs quotes:

"Innovation distinguishes between a leader and a follower"

Authentic Leadership in Action

- *At one and in peace with self*
- *Aligned to purpose for being*
- *Accepting of all human beauty and imperfection*
- *Compassionate and passionate*
- *Audacious*
- *Learners in and of life and love*
- *Creative beyond multi-sensory perception*
- *Define their own destiny and reach it through responsibility and ownership for self*
- *Abundant in energy and every other sense of the richness of life*
- *Humble, patient and attentive*
- *Determined, persistent, tenacious and know no bounds*

The Social Leader

The social leaders are leaders leading for social purpose. They come in all shapes and sizes, guises and titles. My experience throughout the sector has led me to form opinions, which I would dearly like to have challenged. They all face obstacles and how they deal with them depends upon the focus of the organisation they are in.

Quasi-private or quasi-public sector leaders

Quasi-private or quasi-public sector leaders tend to conform to the rules and regulations. They live in a world full of compliance, audit commissions, and accountable spendings. Their funding comes based on the Index of Deprivation or in the case of housing associations, from Governments varying and ever-changing whims about who is responsible for providing social housing and alternatives to service what they have now deemed to be the 'in-betweeners' (those who are not eligible for social housing but are unable to save sufficient to pay a deposit for purchasing a house privately). As such they can get caught up in the plethora of bureaucracy that seems to stifle any amount of audaciousness and creativity. Can they lead differently and beyond the boundaries set to challenge them?

Charity leaders

Charity leaders have a very clearly defined cause and are immensely passionate about it, which narrows their view of the world and can if left unchecked, cause greater dependency than ease suffering. I spoke with the leader of a charity recently who supports people with 'mental difficulties' to create art. In discussing the issue of dependency she admitted that those her charity serves have become dependent upon it, because it is so comfortable for them and a place where they are accepted. She sees the dichotomy in this but doesn't know what to do to change it, or indeed if she should change it.

Community leaders

Community leaders see a wider yet still contextualised picture focusing on the issues prevailing in the community they serve. Some widen their net to learn best practice in other areas that can be translated to their own. Some hook up with other agencies within the community to do joint projects. But like any situation humans face in life, when you're in the midst of it, the boundaries become blurred and they end up helping more and more, losing sight that people need to help themselves.

Speaking with a community development worker recently she was complaining about how many complaints she gets about trivial matters that bog her down in paperwork rather than being out there truly engaging with the community. We talked about the level of burden she was carrying and I asked her how good it made her feel to carry this. She looked at me quizzically and said the tone of my question suggested that she somehow enjoyed it. I asked if she did and together we explored it a little further. She concluded that having people come to her to solve their issues (i.e. the burdens) gave her a sense of importance. It was a reminder that we are all self-reliant and must use our talents to find our own solutions. For her, she realised her talent was hidden because whilst she focused on complaints she could not get on with the facilitation and engagement of community members.

Social Enterprise leaders

Social Enterprise leaders offer business savvy approaches that allow for the promotion of a cause to merge with commercial astuteness so that two audiences become beneficiaries. In a recent survey into social enterprise, 45% of respondents said that 'putting something back into the community' was their reason for setting up a social enterprise.

It may sound strange but my question is what did you take that you have to give back?

I'm sure that this is not the conscious driver for all, however, the scope of operations is mainly very local with two-fifths working in their local area or in one or two local authority areas.

However, one in ten operate on a national scale. And in fact according to data from the Annual Survey of Small Business UK, overall they offer a huge benefit to the UK (aggregated data 2005–07), with approximately 62,000 social enterprises with small and medium social enterprises contributing £24 billion GVA (Gross Value Added) to the UK economy.

Voluntary sector leaders

Voluntary sector leaders encounter barriers and frustrations in relation to funding as in the main they depend entirely on streams of income that are out of their control. These funds pay for the staff they need to run their organisations. And as it doesn't cover it many of the leaders (in smaller organisations) I speak to end up so busy organising and looking after volunteers that there's little time for them to focus on the essence of the delivery. One client organisation who works on behalf of children employs only 20% of the staff that they need to run the organisation, the rest is made up of volunteers. Day to day operations take a huge amount of organisation, effort and reactive management. Whilst leadership is innovative and forward thinking they have the constant over-hang of where the next pennies will come from, which (when they allow and they now know they have the ability) it can slow them down or inhibit them entirely.

I recently asked the leader of a volunteer centre (VC) to run a session with a group of women leaders to talk about what the VC does and how as individuals they could offer their talents to their community. The session was hugely interesting and the women learned that volunteering has far wider opportunities available than they had perceived (one woman had actually said to me at the outset, is she going to talk to us about the soup kitchens!!). The VC leader later told me what her job was really like and whilst she got immense satisfaction from what she does, she spent a significant portion of her time courting funders, selling the idea of volunteering to groups all over her region. Whilst stimulating huge interest, she admitted that the interest was more from organisations seeking volunteers as they didn't have time to manage them, and also had varying degrees of the value they could offer.

The Social Entrepreneur

The Social Entrepreneur with a focus on creating social capital has of all the previous roles the freedom to be more audacious (or do they?). Their approach is to see a wider picture and capitalise on opportunity wherever they can make or take one. They are veraciously ambitious on behalf of the world and so create innovative solutions that can be replicated and scaled to society's most pressing issues. They are passionate change agents in fact game changers who deliberately set out to challenge status-quo. Their view of profit is beyond anything financial, for them it's about value, abundance and richness in life. No is not a word that exists in their vocabulary, neither does failure as they see this as an experience to learn and grow from.

Of all so far, the Social Entrepreneur fits the picture of the Authentic Social Leader most. However, all social leaders, no matter how I have categorised them or expressed my experience, have at heart one basic and fundamental similarity and it is exactly the same as the vision of the social sector... developing and sustaining health and happiness for all humanity.

To really step up to enabling this, each leader in this sector needs to take a good look at the resource they have both within and out with, and start leveraging and expanding upon them more. Paradoxically this world has a wealth of abundant resource yet is in crisis and sees only scarcity.

The authentic social leader has the ability to see the need and galvanise the resources necessary to fulfil the need and in this purpose there is little that stands in their way, other than themselves.

They have no 'comfort zone', every day stretches them deliberately to learn more, be more, and the more they do the easier it becomes. They are at ease with the unknown and know that when they let go of not knowing the knowing has the space to appear. They are at ease in unfamiliarity as they know it expands them.

They have the ability to let go, to make way for new and the faith that the new will bring transformation and evolution.

They follow their own path no one else's as they are creators not sheep. They know and fully accept they will not please all of the people all of the time and they would not aim to as *"in order to please others, we lose our hold on our life's purpose".* (Epictetus)

They are fully aware, conscious and deliberate in their in-fluence and use the power of it to permeate more, role-model the way and demonstrate the change they wish to see.

They trust implicitly knowing they can't give something they have not got and they continuously develop their faith and trust in self. They know it is one of their greatest assets and they use it abundantly.

Exercise Time

How has your life been enriched as a result of what you do?

What is your definition of leadership and how you live this?

What would you say your top ten values or beliefs are?

How do these drive what you do and how you do it?

What does curiosity mean to you and for you?

How often are you curious? How do you use curiosity in your life?

When do you recognise choice and in what ways do you go about exploring choice or the existence of it for you and others?

What do you do to develop awareness of the existence of choice for those you support?

What does giving mean to you?

When you help another, what is the essence of what you are aiming to achieve?

How is it possible to recognise authenticity in yourself and others?

Is it possible for you to always be authentic?

Do you know how to discover your intuitions? In what ways do you do this?

To what extent to do you allow these to guide you?

For you, *is there* any correlation between authenticity and intuition? Can you evoke one without the other?

In what ways can you learn?

In what ways can you change?

In what ways can you actualise?

Action

What have you learned from answering these questions and how will you put this into action?

How more aligned are you than you thought to Authentic Social Leadership and what do you now need to do to become even more aligned?

How will you know when you achieved either of these actions?

Précis

Leadership: A gift we are all endowed with but one that shines when authenticity guides.

In-Fluence: We cannot not influence

Trust! You cannot give something you have not got, if you do not trust yourself you cannot trust another.

Authentic Social Leaders: The belief that all others contain a unique ability of their own and as such, aid them to exploit and expand their own capabilities.

Audaciousness: To eradicate fear of the challenge to pave the way to success.

The Social Leader and Social Leadership

help**Less**

PART TWO

The Human Connection

It is time to stop pleading and start **leading**

CHAPTER FIVE

Every human is human yet we look and behave different

We all had the same parents
many million years ago
why can't we live in freedom
without hunger, with no war

at the beginning we all had
one father and one mother
that's what we're descending from

why so much hate
between races and religions

Enigma, Lyrics of Seven Lives

Wise words from a group that 'get' societal issues to express them through music and lyrics. We seem to have forgotten that we are all the same, we are all human, we all have the same value in the world and every life is significant in its own right. We are all one, and one of all.

We did not just arrive, we evolved

We are all descendant from the same place somewhere back in the history of Earth. Over millions of years we have evolved to become the beings we are today. And although we believe we are highly evolved and the most superior species inhabiting this earth, we are actually the only species that perpetually kill one another every day, judge one another (good/bad, right/wrong, worthy/unworthy, superior/inferior etc.) and cause devastation and destruction to Mother Earth.

Despite our evolved intelligence, education, technological advancements and economic prosperity, we are nonetheless incredibly un-evolved. We believe we've evolved beyond our Neanderthal existence of 'hunter gatherer'. But have we really?

We still hunt out opportunities that effectively feed and clothe us, and we gather material, possessions and education to make us feel like we're evolving (and contributing).

Somewhere along the line though we lost our way and the hunting and gathering was turned inward on ourselves – against one another. We have created weapons of mass-destruction, we war with other humans, we use our beliefs against one another, we suppress our emotions (the feature that when used intelligently differentiates us most from other species) in preference for logic and objectivity and we view materialism as a symbol of success.

The truth is we share 96% of our DNA with chimpanzees, 85% with mice and about 50% with a tree and as humans we share 99.9% of DNA with one another. What has evolved is the order in which the rungs appear in the DNA ladder and as such humans learned to use their hands – the feature that, aside from emotions, has catapulted our evolution beyond the chimpanzee!

The other truth is that there is no such thing as race! Race is biologically real – but there are no genetic markers. Any two individuals within any so-called race may be as different from one another as they are from any other in any so-called race. Eighty-five percent of our genes are exactly the same. Yet somehow in the UK, we'd prefer to leave a child in care rather than allow the child to be adopted by parents of a different colour!

Dr Nina Jablonski has done a vast amount of research on the pigmentation of skin and concludes that this is the key to what we have come to know or label as 'race'. I recommend you watch her presentation on:

http://www.youtube.com/watch?v=d4KcRMTKImQ.

Undoubtedly we have evolved, so why therefore do we live in a world where we have to defend ourselves against one another? Why do we live in a world where some have and some haven't? Why are we living in a world where we have even invented the concept of 'equal' or 'equality'?

Somewhere in your mind, particularly when you are engaged in work of a social nature, you ask yourself these questions daily. I don't personally have the answer to these questions as I know I am not the font of all knowledge. I do, however, have some suggestions to provoke debate and by default therefore our wider thinking.

"All men are created equal"

John Locke

Is this really true in today's society? Obviously I would say it is as I've already demonstrated as humans, we have created an illusion that it isn't!! We develop and implement vast policies, procedures, laws, moral codes and so much more to promote the concept of equity. But has any of it created any equity?

The upshot is that we operate on a 'Politically Correct' basis not on a human level of respecting the uniqueness of every individual. It has become a political rather than heart motivated approach based on judgement and a concept of 'rightness' or 'wrongness'.

What does 'equal' really mean?

Dictionary definitions of 'equal' does not actually recognise the uniqueness of individuals in that it categorises in terms of ability, quality, standing and measure. It makes no allowance for sameness, difference or uniqueness. Equity is defined as fairness or conformity with rules or standards. But who makes the rules or standards, who determines what is meant by fairness? Again judgement based perceptions!

By equality, I mean everyone having an equal chance in life so that, regardless of background or circumstance, every individual can contribute to society, fulfil their potential and live a satisfying life. Therefore we will each live life in our own unique way mutually respecting both our sameness and difference and the uniqueness of the contribution each of us can make. The key to 'equal' or 'equity' is acceptance.

What do I mean by acceptance? Acceptance is born from self. When we reach a point where we can accept self fully and completely without judgement then and only then can we begin the process of accepting others. As humans we make sense of the world only by comparison and as such we always seek outside for validity of our beingness. Until the point of self-acceptance we will continue to be affected by the views, opinions and judgement of others. When we stop being affected by others we naturally view ourselves as being equal – a no more or no less being where difference and sameness merely offer complementariness.

Earlier (in chapter 3 The Social/Third Sector) I referred to a youth initiative and a young boy asking if he was deprived. Up to over hearing the telephone conversation he had not considered himself to be unequal to anyone else in any way. He had also not considered there to be inequities between him and the wider world or that there were less opportunities for him. He was living his life, his way, happily and healthily.

It was through our intervention that he began to think differently. This could be seen as useful in raising his personal awareness, conversely it could also be an unhelpful one. Either way, in this case it was judgementally based – or politically based!

A Human Being is different to a Human Doing

What enables a person to reach a point of acceptance is creating sufficient space for reflection in their life. Space to allow the constant chatter of the brain to stop comparing, to be inward with self to allow a beingness rather than a doingness.

Reflection Time

How often *do you spend time with just yourself?*

How aware *are you of what your body is telling you?*

Do you *enjoy your own company and are you at peace in it?*

Do you *ever stop and I mean truly stop, with no activity, no television, no reading, no listening to music, no knitting, ironing, exercise or anything else to occupy you?*

How often *do you allow your mind to clear to allow space for you to hear your inner wisdom and guidance?*

*Beyond this **can you** allow your mind to clear even more to enter into a space of nothingness?*

Many of the leaders I work with look at me like I'm some sort of crazy chick when I ask these questions. Some think that it is all a bit too 'ethereal' or a bit 'way out there'. And why is this?

Because to most, it is new, it is unfamiliar, it is scary and it doesn't seem to 'fit' with an organisational context. There are generally two stock responses to these questions (or variations on a theme). Did you answer with either one of these?

"But what if I don't like what I find?"

or

"I haven't got time for such frivolity and fluffiness!"

This is not as some would deem it 'spiritual stuff', there is without doubt a logic behind it. Without spending this quality time with self, how can you offer quality time to another? If you don't enjoy your own company and be at peace with you how can you with another? If you haven't reached a point of self-acceptance how can you accept another?

We cannot give what we haven't got!!!

If you never stop to recognise the beauty around you, or gifts bestowed upon you, appreciate the miracle of your body as a vehicle for your being on this earth, you live a life of pure existence or as I call it 'the waking dead'.

As a nation or indeed a human race the vast majority just exist from day-to-day. Each day like the previous, each moment passing by without cognisance whilst our mind wanders to what happened in the past and what may happen in the future. Forgetting all the while that now is present (a gift) and that will never ever come again. We hanker after tomorrow but tomorrow never comes because it's today!

These gems of realisation are the key to living or existing.

The Thrive, Survive or Dive Options for Life

Consciously or not, we all make a choice in our life as to whether we thrive, survive or dive. Which have you chosen?

The Thrive Option

A thriving option is evoked when you decide to take ownership of your own life connecting with who you are and allowing yourself to live the fullness of you. A journey of awakening will have occurred to raise your awareness to you developing a loving accepting relationship with yourself. In doing so you will know that every experience you've ever had, good or bad, is all part of the awakening process and all designed to enable your recognition of the power contained within and the depth of resources you have available to you and for you.

This awakening process can happen at any age, it is not reserved or preserved and it's a lifelong journey of constant evaluation and re-evaluation. Every day new experiences are brought to awaken further. Every day your senses learn anew and more. Every day the scope of vision, imagination and intuition broadens and new possibilities open (in adversity or otherwise) as Maxi Jazz put it: *"you don't need eyes to have vision".* Every day is a gift for which you take time to offer gratitude and appreciation.

You are doing what makes you come alive and so you no longer think about it as 'work'. What you do may well make you a lot of money, or may not. Either way you're not doing it for money, you're doing it because you are completely aligned to it and it to you. Your needs and desires are met, you are living a fulfilled life and happiness is innate within. You have reached a point where it's no longer important to be liked by others, but it is hugely important to be able to live with yourself.

Please know that this is not an idealised life, it is real to the person living it. They are still offered immense challenges but they handle them with grace and ease knowing they have capacity to move through and beyond.

Thrive Option in Action

A friend, fellow journey person and teacher was diagnosed with cancer in 2007. It was in her skin. A wife and mother of four children ranging from 4-14 in her late thirties, this was a shock. But as a master of the thrive option, she dealt with it amazingly, seeking new learning in her experience and sharing with others whatever she gained both through her pain and the process of physical change to her body. Each day she inspired those around her as she continued to be as graceful and beautiful in her outlook and approach as she always had been. In the depths of her pain, all she offered was love and reassurance to all those around her that all was OK no matter the outcome. Her strength and determination touched even the most unawakened of hearts.

In the summer of 2010, she took her leave from one of her life's passions (teaching children) to spend quality time with her other life passions – herself and her family. She knew she was dying so took the time to arrange her funeral so that her message could continue beyond her mortal life. In August 2010, the crematorium was packed out as friends, colleagues, neighbours, students, and those she'd touched came to celebrate her life. At her request everyone wore green or silver, including her husband who'd sprayed his hair.

In her life my friend took the option to thrive and no matter the length of her life or the challenges she faced her option remained resolute. She leaves that legacy for her children and for all those she touched along the way.

The survive option is one filled with busyness. Planful and ambitious in your approach you set about creating the perfect life for yourself, the one that has the perfect job, home, family, wife/husband, car, holidays etc. You've set out your plans of what you want to achieve and acquire and each time you reach one you tick the box and move on to the next. You are busy climbing the ladder of success, networking, educating yourself and making yourself rather indispensible. Status is important to you and in the hierarchy you absolutely aim to reach the top.

Similarly in your social standing you are seen in the right places, with the right people and make time wherever you can to fit in friends, family and sometimes (albeit rare) that treat for yourself such as the gym or a game of golf.

You have occasional flashes of inspiration of getting out there and becoming your own boss but somehow there's always a reason why you can't pursue, such as the good salary or pension you're currently on. Some do become their own boss but end up working just as many hours as before as it turns out their boss is more of a tyrant than their previous one!!

Everything is ahead of you, out there yet to be achieved. You may occasionally allow yourself to recognise what you've already achieved but only to check your journey is heading firmly to the destination you've outlined.

But no matter what you achieve, somehow the pleasure you thought you'd gain from it doesn't materialise, so you head for bigger and better things. You seek even further recognition. You can stretch thinking and you can and do create your life in so many ways, but there are limitations. These limitations contain market forces, economic circumstance, what others think or perceive of you, health and education.

In reality the survive option is living in existence, caught up in the humdrum of the life and the expectations of what success is, not really connected to who you are or to the beauty and love that surrounds you.

Survive Option in Action

A client came to me a year ago, we'll call him Tony. I asked him what had brought him to me and what he wanted to gain from coaching. He looked very perplexed and said he really wasn't sure and in fact was quite embarrassed to be there. I gave him space and eventually he said that for the past year each day he awoke the first thought on his mind was "there's something missing". For a year Tony had been analysing his life and rationally and logically he could not answer the question. He'd attempted so many times to put it aside as there clearly wasn't anything missing according to his analysis. But something nagged at him persistently and so finally he'd decided to seek assistance to broaden his thinking, hence arriving at my door.

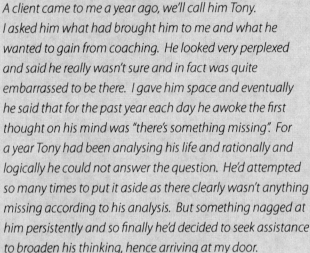

In his mid-teens Tony had made his career choice and from here had mapped out his life. Three major things that he wanted to achieve included reaching an executive position by the time he was 30, marrying and having children. The rest he believed would drop in around it. Here

he was now in his early thirties, having achieved exactly
what he'd set out to achieve and more; a great house; two
cars; annual holidays (sometimes twice); a good network
around him; the occasional game of golf and pint with the
boys, and respect for his knowledge in his field.

It made no sense to him that he should feel like
something was missing and worse he felt guilty for feeling
this way when he knew (for him) that he had a life that
most would be hugely envious of.

After 3 sessions Tony knew exactly what was missing
and laughed heartily when he realised because it was just
so simple.

Tony was missing himself!!

Through the sessions but mainly outside of them, Tony
became an observer of himself and his emotions. He would
stop several times a day and just check in with himself
(mind, body and soul) and ask, where am I now, how do I
feel and why is this?

Armed with awareness and recognition of his
emotion and the developing ability to make meaning of
it for himself, Tony moved on to the next stage of looking
inward, creating space for him to just be. Ultimately Tony
freed himself of the trap of living his life for others realising
that when he wasn't happy he couldn't make anyone
else happy. More than that he realised he didn't have the
capacity ever to make another happy…happiness comes
from within. He can but influence!

The Dive Option

As you can imagine the dive option is a pure existence option. Each day it offers more challenges and struggles and you wonder when you will be free of it all. You dream of winning the lottery so that you can change your life and not have to work so hard. You are subject to anything and everything that happens in your external environment.

Life is just done to you and you have little or no choice in what happens. Almost victim like, some days you just want to give up. No matter how many people are around you, you still feel isolated. You look forward to weekends when you can let your hair down but they come and go so quick. You feel tired most of the time and you suffer from ailment after ailment. You do what your doctor tells you but you never seem to fully recover. You give over your power to the experts and hope that they will save you.

Your conversation with others is a mutual unburdening of the trials and tribulations of life. You feel better for a while when you know you're not suffering alone but it's short-lived as you go back to heaviness of life. You watch soap operas and television in general and take a keen interest in others lives to drown out living your own.

You are subject to the opinions of others and are on a constant quest to be acknowledged and accepted, so you follow the trends wherever possible and do what is expected of you. You have some good days and for the most part you put on a brave face.

A Dive Option in Action

There are many levels to the dive option, here's just one:

A gentleman, call him Harry aged 47. Harry had a reasonable childhood with the exception that he looked different to most in his community (because of his race!), but a really lovely guy he managed to overcome and make some great friends. After an apprenticeship at the age of 18 he joined the workforce.

Harry entered his first serious relationship at the age of 20; at 23 his girlfriend arrived home out of the blue and said she didn't love him any longer. She left and within a year she was married with a child. Harry was distraught and vowed never to give his heart away again. Two years later determinedly single, he met another woman and after a year they moved in together.

Each day Harry did his job, did what he was told and every few years got a pay rise for his efforts. His relationship seemed great to the outside world, yet inside it was difficult as neither one seemed wholly capable of truly engaging, but after 8 years together they decided to tie the knot.

Things got worse after that and Harry had a major crisis of confidence, his wife seemed to make matters worse so left to give him space to 'find himself.' They got back together but it was never the same. Harry functioned in everyday life but was disconnected, lost somewhere in a void.

Dreadfully unhappy in his job where he was perpetually treated appallingly despite his now 20 years of service there was little in his life to give him pleasure. At 44 another serious crisis and Harry just didn't want to be on this earth plane any longer, he left his 14 year relationship with his wife. He very quickly hooked up with another but says it's still not right. He continues in his job only because he has no idea what else he could do and hey, it pays him a wage.

Harry is a persistent victim of circumstance, environment and everyone else's feelings. He lives with guilt, shame and remorse and having tried counselling feels that this is just the life he is destined to live, so he wears a mask and gets on.

What I have presented in each of these options is an extreme form. Within each there are many different levels and an individual may ebb and flow within each through different stages in their life. However, in the main each option is a state of mind and a state of being.

We are all both leaders and followers

We tend to have a preference or leaning toward one or the other, and this determined by the option we make in thriving, surviving or diving.

Ultimately the point of highlighting the options of thrive, survive and dive is to demonstrate that we live life either at effect or at cause. At effect we are or become the effect of everything that goes on outside or around us as in the case of either the survive or dive option. Alternatively we can live life at cause, which is when we accept that we are the cause of how we live our lives i.e. self-ownership.

As can be seen from the examples, experiences difficult or not, can be used to evolve or dissolve us. We all have the power within to decide which. In countries much poorer than the UK the same principles apply and the poorest of the poor can still thrive making the best use of anything and everything they can access. There are examples all around us if we care to look. Paradoxically we will only ever see that which we know so if I'm in a dive option I will resonate readily with others in this place.

Our social structures are built around these options and those most likely to access the services of the social sector will have a survive or dive option. As a social leader or contributor to the sector we must first know what option we have made as that's the one we'll be modelling!!

And we are the teachers. But are we aware of what we are teaching?

It is not that some are not taught, it is that they are taught!

As with my friend, she has taught her children to thrive, despite them losing their mother at such tender ages. Tony was taught to be successful but by someone else's standards or judgement of what success looked like. And Harry was taught that life is hard and true love doesn't really exist.

Our media also teaches us immensely – is it for our benefit? Everyday we are exposed to massive amounts of media, branding, and illusions of what can make us happy. We buy more and more in the vain hope it will provide happiness, health, stress relief, the answer to our prayers. It will make us look younger, better looking, slimmer, trendier, more intelligent. It will win us friends, that promotion, that holiday that promises to fulfil our fantasy. We don't buy a product or service, we buy the promise of what it will give us. Today we look for the overnight solution, the quick wins or a quick fix.

The media influence our lives immeasurably. Every morning we can put the news on and hear of all the hell that's happening, the doom and gloom of another recession, another cutback, more jobs lost, more people killed. Every night before we go to bed, more bad news. It's inevitable that whatever is happening will eventually effect us so we passively wait for it to hit or we take some actions to protect what we have worked so hard for.

Reflection Time

An American psychiatrist did a rather unethical study of his patients. For six months as they came to see him he would consistently use words like; grey, old, slow, forgetful, tired, lethargic, powerless, victim, down, suppressed, bad, heavy etc. Without fail throughout the months his patients deteriorated and walked slower and slower from his office, dragging their tired bodies and reporting how heavy they felt.

For the next six months with the same patients he used words like; young, energetic, high, fast, positive, good, virile, strong, happy, light, powerful etc. His patients improved dramatically almost skipping out of his office. They started experiencing opportunities open up in their lives they could never have imagined. They were upbeat and positive about themselves and others and most discharged themselves.

The point of offering this story is to raise your awareness of what you do to yourself by watching the news before you leave your home in the morning and then again before you go to bed every night!!

We are an effect of our media so choosing what we watch and listen to, or observe on our travels may be a good place to start.

Greed has consumed our lives and the only way that we have to wake up to this is to force ourselves into a recession position that makes us take notice. According to David Cameron in an interview with Andrew Marr (03/10/10 BBC1), we're now entering what's been called a double-dip recession. In other words we haven't learned enough and we need to challenge ourselves even more?

It seems we're never enough just as we are and so are always striving to have more in the hope that it makes us happy or makes us more!! We've made life all about the destination and we've forgotten how to appreciate the journey. Our goals are made up of acquisition or achievement, there's nothing about living or being!!

We are living unsustainably and the bubble has finally burst, we now have to learn to become enough.

Précis

Evolution: To continuously learn from our experiences to grow and enrich self and humanity.

Equality: Every being can contribute to society, and ultimately attain a satisfying life not just an existence.

Thrive: To take ownership of your own life, be self-determining and directing.

Survive: An ambitious approach to your life in order to fulfill security and acceptance.

Dive: Present living to overcome day-to-day challenges in the need just to survive.

Media: Hypnotises us!

help**Less**

PART THREE

The Adaptive™

It is time to stop pleading and start **leading**

CHAPTER SIX

Introduction to
The Adaptive ™

The birthing of my learning

Even as a child I was fascinated by human behaviour and psychology. I used to sit in my mother's car whilst she ran in and out of suppliers purchasing materials for the business that she and my dad ran. I never really noticed time disappear whilst I watched people's comings and goings. Even whilst we were driving I'd watch people at traffic lights with interest. I always wondered where everyone was going and what their life offered different to mine. Moreover I marvelled at how busy everyone was, rare actually did I see many smile as they walked. That seemed to only occur when in interaction with another.

Coming from a relatively large Irish catholic family, as kids we looked after one another so my eldest sister had quite a parental role with my siblings and I, and when she left home not long after my youngest brother came along I took on a parental role. I learned early on, the power of nurturing and the responsibility of 'looking after' another.

By the time I reached my teens I was completely lost, totally passive in the world and a victim in so many ways. I'd gone to school at a mixed secondary comprehensive but coming from a private estate in a house that my father had built for us, I was constantly chastised for being 'Posh'. That coupled with the fact that I had been born in London and therefore to my fellow students a 'Brit' in Dublin Ireland, isolated me hugely. Looking back now it was amazing learning for me.

Due to recession and the fact that I just couldn't 'find' myself, I left Ireland in my late teens and returned to live in London. Oddly enough there I was considered Irish by everyone I met, which confused me more!!

I struck gold with a temporary job that turned permanent and was quickly offered the opportunity to learn the entire business, just like a graduate trainee although I had no such education. Exposed to every department within the company I marvelled at the difference in personality from one department to another and within that their outlook of their customer (internal or external).

In my personal life I was in the midst of a violent marriage that led me in to severe debt and eventually homeless despite my really great job! Homelessness was actually a safer option for me at the time. However, my local council took little of this on board and basically said if my life was in danger they would suggest I book a flight on his credit card and go back to Ireland where I belonged!!!

The second council took three months to pour over all my financials, every GP record that recorded my health over the previous five years, interviews about my life to ensure consistency and prove that I was worthy of being housed. Eventually they offered me a flat that had been released that day following a case to prove the double-rape and double-murder that had occurred in it. I remember still vividly, arriving at the same time as a whole load of people in white jumpsuits entered to clean it up. The blood had stained into and was ingrained in the concrete floor, splashing all up the walls. I was physically sick whilst the housing officer was telling me all the reasons I couldn't reject the offer of this 'home'.

Again for me homelessness was the safer option. But a friend who volunteered at the battered wives home in Chiswick asked her partner (a formidable journalist) to write a letter for me. I brought it the following day to the council and sat waiting for 3 hours. To this day I do not know what was written but I got another offer a week later which was in a secure building manned by a concierge. The housing officer releasing the property said to me: *"I don't know how you did this but I have to tell you, you will be absolutely grateful for this and know that you owe this country. It's only because you're Irish that you got it."*

I stayed there for a year working hard to get my financial situation under control. At rock-bottom I knew the only way was up and onwards. Somewhere within me also, I knew that I had created this situation and I was the only one now who could get me out of it.

And I did, a year later I had completely transformed my life. I moved north, got a new job, entered into third education and engaged in a new relationship.

In this place I gave myself the freedom to explore my journey and how I had come to have allowed the world to do to me. I also started to study people again and in doing so, studied me!

The Birthing of The Adaptive™

A decade and a half later, having worked across industries and varying economic and social environments directly with people, it all finally came together for me. A friend and I had taken ourselves out of the busyness of life to stop and reflect on what we'd learned in our lives and what we were doing to apply our learning and share it with others.

After a morning of walking, talking, drinking coffee and soaking up the atmosphere of Holy Island (Northumberland), without consciousness I expressed a four-component model. It made sense really as a huge amount of management and leadership theory was presented in a four-box model. But there was something not sitting right, not least that this was definitely not a 'model'.

Over the next month I played with it. The components were right but still something was missing. I was on a retreat and in one of the workshops a woman was talking about what she called 'The Diamond Light'. Astonished a friend and I sat listening to the words of this woman. Almost everything I'd written in the previous month was being expressed from this woman's mouth. It was like she was inside my head and heart. I had to have a coffee with her.

An hour and a half later, several light bulb moments and it was clear what was missing. This wasn't just a four-box square this was a diamond. An oscillating octahedron.

The Adaptive^{TM} Diamond

In geometry, an octahedron (plural: octahedra) is a polyhedron with eight faces. A polyhedron is a geometric solid in three dimensions with flat faces and straight edges. Natural crystals of diamond, alum or fluorite are commonly octahedral.

The octahedron is a symmetrical eight sided shape that may look like two four sided pyramids lying base to base. But closer inspection will show that each set of opposing points is

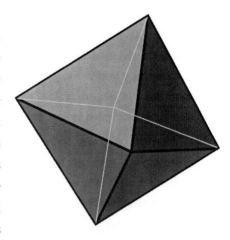

exactly the same and could serve equally well as the 'top' and 'bottom' of the two pyramids. In fact there is no top or bottom on isometric forms. The faces are equilateral triangles unless modified. There are six points, eight faces and twelve edges. Each face is parallel to the opposite face. The octahedron is related to the cube by placing each point of an octahedron at the centre of each face of a cube.

Diamond is the ultimate gemstone, it has many strengths and few weaknesses. The diamond is the hardest substance found in nature, in fact four times harder than the next hardest natural mineral, corundum (sapphire and ruby). However, hard as it is, it is not incapable of being penetrated. Diamond has four directions of cleavage, meaning that if it receives a sharp blow in one of these directions it will cleave, or split.

As a gemstone, the diamond's single flaw (perfect cleavage) is far outweighed by the sum of its positive qualities. It has a broad colour range, high refraction, high dispersion or fire, very low reactivity to chemicals, rarity, and of course, extreme hardness and durability.

In terms of its physical properties, the diamond is the ultimate mineral in several ways: hardness; clarity; thermal conductivity; melting point; lattice density; tensile density, and compressive strength.

But why am I telling you this? Because for me everything that is the octahedron and diamond is reflective in any human. We also have many strengths and few weaknesses. We are also hard but not impenetrable, and whatever our flaws they are also far outweighed by our positive qualities.

Further we are without doubt multi-faceted, multi-dimensional, with no top or bottom to our being and as important each face we put on is parallel to the opposite face. In other words we reflect and project everything we're about in the world.

Finally we are never fixed in the world either, as energy beings we are motion and therefore oscillating.

The Concept of The Adaptive™

It is my observation that life throws us challenge and stimulation every day. How we handle this depends on how stable we are in our core (at our centre, the heart of us, the essence of who we are). In other words how 'at home' we are in our own being.

In my teens and early twenties I did not cope with the challenges of life particularly well and in fact I have come to believe that my unstableness within probably led to the depth of challenge I was offered. I have no proof for such a hypothesis apart from knowing I face a very different set of challenges today, which are more energising and aligned to my purpose for being.

In my life today I feel balanced within and no matter what I face outside, I know that creating a little space for me to be, brings me back into balance and harmony. I'm further amazed at the amount of people that I have around me who are just like this. Like attracts like, or so the saying goes.

However, I am startlingly aware, particularly working in the social sector that a huge amount of the population are not balanced, and are not aligned to their purpose for being. Hence energy is drained rather than created, time goes fast or slow and life is an existence rather that something to behold in love and beauty.

Why is this? There are a multitude of answers to this, a huge amount of which have already been discussed in previous chapters. But resoundingly, no matter the manifestation, there is one thing that stands out above everything else:

the ability to really connect with, and be with, self

So many people that I work with realise once they commence that in fact they don't really know themselves. They've never taken the time to get to know themselves. They've never really spent time with themselves. They have never really explored what makes them light up and come alive. They have never actually said to themselves, I love me. They have never acknowledged the tremendous talent, knowledge, knowing, loving that exists within them. Modesty keeps them grounded!

We live in an incredibly modest society where if we were to acknowledge such things we would be perceived as being arrogant or egoful. But as I have persistently said throughout, we cannot give what we haven't got. If I can't move myself to acknowledge my talents how can I truly embrace them in another.

It's what I call the mirror effect. In other words we reflect and project everything we're about in the world.

So conversely not acknowledging is the egoful thing. Not acknowledging is arrogant.

In Action

In support of Peace One Day's day of Peace I had organised some events in the North-East of England. I received a telephone call from a seventeen year old girl who had also organised an event in the same region for the same cause who thought that we should join forces. I loved the idea and got together with her to discuss it. During the conversation about world peace and her purpose in life and how she was living this, quite matter of fact the girl said: "God has gifted me with beauty and so I am going to become a famous model and from that platform spread the word of peace."

There was no shame, modesty or arrogance in this seventeen year old beautiful soul, just a pureness of heart and a complete acknowledgement of the gifts she had to bring to bear in this world.

Secondly, even if we didn't believe this and actually we do acknowledge and embrace everything about self, the next barrier is our busyness. We couldn't be perceived to be lazy so we must at least look busy, which in reality is just us avoiding being with self!!

I've been speaking with a number of colleagues recently who are amazing high energy beings but somehow are going through a shift. The shift for them has been about allowing themselves to fully experience their emotion, to be with self, to not move to busy themselves with something else, to not be afraid that the emotion will somehow kill them if they just let it be!!

When they do stop; when they do allow the absolute experience of the emotion; when they can just be with self without moving, they find an inner peace and a space of freedom and of liberation of all fear. Going into the emotion is not what kills. Suppressing, depressing, avoiding, denying the emotion is the slow and painful death of the soul. It is also the beginnings of dis-ease in the body.

Balance can only come when you're willing to let go. Alignment can only come when you know who you are and can live your life in synchronicity with self.

Oscillation is the added dimension

When you get both balance and alignment you can oscillate wherever you want and therefore be 'Adaptive' readily capable of adjusting, modifying, amending to whatever comes your way. The key here is that you can come back to your own balance whenever you want – adapting being temporal. And what allows this is the deep grounding of your balance and alignment with self?

In oscillation you can move into anyone else's space without compromise to you, without sacrifice to you, without judgement to them or you. From this place you can build deep rapport with another, you can be truly compassionate with another and you can see the world through their eyes. And all of this, you can do without detriment to you or the other person.

The things I have seen in decades of deliberate observation

I've been privileged in my career to have experienced so many different industries, leaders, sectors and both economic and social environments. Here are some common themes that I recognised within them. I would also quantify that of course in all of these experiences, there were those that didn't portray the degree of fear I'm about to mention and we'll talk about how this manifests later.

In my career I worked in leisure, tourism, construction, manufacturing, professional services, pharmaceutical, security industry and many more. Nearly every leader I met was motivated by fear. The first of their fears was financial, could they bring in enough money, was the business financially stable, was it competitive enough, was it profitable enough, could they take the salary that was commensurate with the lifestyle that a leader should have!!

The second of their fears was failure. So intense was this feeling that some spent their life in work, with little time for anything or anyone else. They took responsibility for everything that happened, making themselves indispensable to the point they couldn't take any time off and no one could make a decision without them. The stick they wielded was one filled with hard work, responsibility and burden for the business.

In Action

When business wasn't good for whatever reason the first thing I heard from leaders was "we need to downsize". I ran so many downsize programmes on behalf of organisations in my early career that in the period of 5 years through recession I personally managed 10,000+ redundancies. It was the answer to everything. It was the immediate and short-sighted answer. It was the answer to getting rid of all the ones that hadn't been managed effectively. It was the answer to keeping business going, saving financially and not failing. Yet it rarely was!

I then went on to work in the social sector with a variety of organisations. Here I found commonality in the leaders again. Financial concern was deeply embedded here too but now it was about where they got funding, how they would pay for the type of projects they really wanted to do. But this fear was not as great as their fear of failure. In the social sector I found even more personal accountability for apparent failures. Much greater sticks were being wielded here that hit them with guilt, shame and worthlessness. All the responsibility for others lay firmly on their shoulders.

In Action

An organisation I have worked with formed itself into a group so that it could ethically earn money to pay for the 'charity' elements of what it did. It was left to get on and do what it needed to do to produce funding for the remainder of the business, however, commercial astuteness was not its focus. Some years later and it is in a financial crisis that has been ignored by the board of the group because they are afraid to 'let people down' by making the necessary changes that are required to refocus the organisation. The guilt and shame of managing people and perhaps even letting go of some in order to take on the talent it requires is just too much for these leaders. They risk losing all by not taking the decisions necessary for the greater good of the whole.

I worked in a Carers Centre directly with carers and gained close access and insight to what made them tick. Here I discovered that many of the carers saw their 'cared for' as victims, victims that they had responsibility for. These carers compromised their lives hugely to be in constant service to the 'victim'. Guilt, shame and worthlessness was not a stick to be wielded, it was just a way of being!!

In Action

One woman in her mid-seventies was looking after her daughter who had a condition that wasn't recognised by the medical profession (ME). Her whole life was lived around her daughter. Any time she organised to go out, even if just for an hour, her daughter would suddenly be really ill and need her full attention. Caught between a rock and a hard place the guilt would keep her present yet the resentment she felt was so overwhelming she'd become ashamed of herself. To compensate she would over-nurture her daughter, doing things for her that she was able to do for herself just to make up for the thoughts and feelings she was experiencing. A perpetuation…

I also worked as a counsellor for a year in a GP's surgery in an area, deemed by the Indices of Deprivation to be a disadvantaged and desolate area. What I discovered about working with GPs was that they were the 'experts' and the 'owner' of patients. In other words, it was their responsibility to diagnose a patient with little information and then set about 'fixing' them. If the patient didn't get 'fixed' the GP would refer them to another 'expert' who would then own the patient from that point on. As a counsellor I found this incredibly difficult as I could not for a moment conceive of being the expert to another human's life. Stick wielded in this environment included guilt, burden, blame, entrenched and bound.

In Action

Each time a new patient was referred to me I would receive their full medical record and was required to read it before meeting with the patient. Firstly I had no idea what any of the 'medical' terminology meant and secondly I did not ever want to be influenced by this data before meeting a client (I couldn't bring myself to call them patients). Thirdly I never saw those I worked with as patients, to me they were people.

I remember reading one lady's notes which told of her regular 'no shows' for appointments and low and behold she didn't show for our first appointment. I persisted and personally called her.

When she finally did arrive I asked her what had brought her. She said that each time she was referred somewhere else there was the promise that this expert would fix her, but she had been perpetually disappointed as to date no one had succeeded.

Attending an appointment with me was different as in our conversation on the phone I had told her my role was not to fix her, I was merely there to help her help herself. This is what compelled her to attend. This woman had spent 6 years working with a psychiatrist in a specialist hospital for mental illness. Personally as with all those I worked with there, I never saw a condition or 'mental' issue, I saw a person, a human being.

As two humans we worked together and two months, eight hours later this woman's physical condition had eased and almost healed. She was sleeping for the first time in thirty years, she had taken control of her life, she was manifesting the dreams she'd had as a child of being a writer and she was being the most amazing mother to her eighteen year old adopted child. She was letting her free and no longer holding her just because she had the condition of Down's Syndrome. She now too saw beyond to the person, the human in her daughter!

All of these situations have EGO in common, all of them needed validation and needed to be needed, all of them judged that they knew best on behalf of another!!

Reflection Time

"But that's not my problem," came the voice of the Chief Executive. "Where does it belong?" I replied. A blank expression met me; a searching for sometime that seemed incomprehensible. Minutes of silence ensued as the search continued and finally the response was "I really don't know". And genuinely there was no knowing left.

Have you ever found yourself in this position? As the leader of a business you are apparently all knowing, all owning and all responsible. And this being the case it's a lonely road you travel with many heavy burdens to carry. If you ever feel like this, the bad news is that you're definitely not alone. The good news is that you therefore don't need to travel alone and the even better news is that actually you don't need to carry the burdens!!

What makes us believe we're alone is that ultimately the buck stops with us, and therefore the decisions we make are vital to success. Furthermore the burdens we carry are the responsibilities for decisions, strategies, operations, the people within and outside the organisation, the suppliers, clients and an endless list of other things...

And what makes us believe this is the case is the illusion that is our EGO (or as Robert Holden explains it – Everything Good Outside or Edging Good Out). Our Ego is our conditioned self, which runs all the programmes that are outside of us to enable conformity, acceptability, relativity, and comparability. So success is outside of us and becomes a measure against something else, a standard somewhere of what I have come to believe as reality.

As a leader therefore my Ego asks of me to seek (the appearance of) greatness, success and financial abundance, then I will be acceptable, then the world will look at me and see I am capable of great things and then I will have arrived. But where will I have arrived, am I not already here? The illusion is that I'm not here, that I still need to journey and that I am on my own in my journey as it's me, as the leader, that others are looking at. It's me that makes this organisation successful or not, therefore it's me that must carry the burdens of responsibility for the organisation and people I serve. Is this a selfless or selfish stance to take, or both?

This illusion is what stifles business, the belief that there is only one leader, the belief that without me, ultimately the business no longer exists. And if you believe this, then it is true. Unconsciously you will take all the major decisions, set the direction, solve the problems, be the inspirer. You will be the role model of the epitome of what leadership means to this organisation. The culture of it will morph itself around you and your style, and finally the organisation will become your 'mini-me'. And all the while you will continue to frustrate yourself at why no one else takes responsibility, why you have to give so much time and effort to everything and everyone, and still do your day job.

The reality is though that you have disempowered all else, unwittingly you have become the 'controller' and no one else knows how to drive!!!

So if you find yourself weighed down by the burdens that leadership brings the first thing to do is just check you're still breathing, and then just stop. Even for five minutes to check in with your inner-self to ask beyond your Ego; what is it you are really doing; what is it you really want, and for what purpose do you really want it? Then if you're feeling brave, ask for some feedback to check the level of empowerment you encourage and allow. Consider your succession, even if just to take a holiday.

The beauty of Ego is its need for connection and relativity and as the saying goes "No Man is an Island". Human beings do not thrive when isolated from others and therefore as a leader you have abundant capacity to thrive and perform at your ultimate when you use resource around you. Enable your people to believe in their ability to achieve the outcomes you collectively want **for the organisation, for your patients/client's health**, albeit they may undertake them in a different manner. Solicit their opinions and ideas, you never know you might learn something or at least have your perspective widened.

Remember unless you specifically want to be a sole-trader in which case the organisation lives and dies as you do… YOU are not the organisation, the organisation is not you. The organisation is an entity in and of itself and as the leader you are its servant, serve it to the best of your ability using your talents to lift and encourage others into their own power to facilitate the ongoing future of the organisation and those it serves.

Paula McCormack
Leadership or Egoship

Article Published North East Times

Everything is on the Go…Pace of Living is Frightening

Earlier in this chapter I mentioned that busyness is a reason not to really get to know self. We live in a society where everything is action, everything is on the go, so much is marketed and packaged for the 'on the go' lifestyle.

We have untold amounts of 'fast-food' establishments. 'McDonalds' is apparently the largest franchise in the world, with 'Subway' taking a very close second. Then there are the coffee joints and I'm sure if you took just a second you could name at least three different ones that can be found on your high street. Supermarkets prepare ready-made meals to just microwave and go.

We have ipads, ipods, notebooks, phones with internet, digital book readers and gaming technology, all of which have changed the art of conversation. We and certainly the next generations communicate through facebook, twitter, online gaming, text and other social media without ever having to physically meet with another.

Yet Match.com report that 17% of couples married since 2006/7, or 1 in 6, met each other on an online dating site (survey 2009/2010). What kind of relationships are we building?

In the US, 1 in 2 marriages end in divorce, and in the UK it is one in every three (the UK being the highest in Europe). According to Channel 4's "21st Century Family" in 2005 when figures lay at two in five British marriages ending in divorce, this was costing the British tax payer an estimated £15 billion a year with untold sociological repercussions. Financial problems are cited as the main concern of many couples who are struggling and trying to balance a home life when both are working, or worse both are out of jobs. Other reasons are poor communication, a lack of commitment to the marriage, infidelity, a change in priorities, addictions/substance abuse, physical/sexual abuse, and finally, a lack of conflict resolution skills.

Essentially we don't have time to invest in relationships, in each other, in family, in being with one another just for the sake of being with one another, or love!

Reflection Time

Office of National Statistics UK Social Trends No. 37 2007 Edition

Nearly a quarter (24%) of children lived with just one parent last year, three times the proportion recorded in 1972.

Lone-parent families are three times more likely to live in rented accommodation than couples with children.

In 2005, 66% of single-parent families lived in rented housing compared with 22% of couples with dependent children.

More than half (52%) of them rented in the social sector compared with 14% of two-parent families.

Lone-parent families are also more likely to live in "non-decent" homes, according to the ONS.

In 2004, 29% of lone-parent households with children lived in buildings which did not meet certain minimum standards, compared with 23% of "couple households."

Since 1971 the proportion of all people living in "traditional" family households of couples with dependent children has fallen from 52% to 37%.

Nine out of 10 lone-parent families are headed by mothers.

Children are increasingly technology-savvy, with around 50% of eight to eleven year olds having their own mobile phone.

Shockingly I've heard it said: *"There are ready-made families out there for the taking and as a woman I don't have to create my own it's already there, why should I mess with my body for a child or wait 9 months."*

Despite recession we still don't have to wait to save up for the things we want today. I can still have a store card, a credit card, or buy now pay later on electrical or furnishing goods.

Patience is a virtue but tomorrow never comes

Précis

Concept of The Adaptive™ : Approach is in essence to discover who you really are and choose the way you wish to live and be in your life.

EGO: The ultimate human element that requires acceptance of self from others.

Mirror Effect: "Everything I see is a mere reflection of me." We reflect and project everything we are about in the world.

Every-thing is on the go: Which means we haven't time to stop and be or listen to me.

Introduction to
The Adaptive ™

CHAPTER SEVEN

The Adaptive™ Approach

A move towards realising your true potential

My whole life even back to my childhood as I've already described has been in the service of people. In my career, even back to when I was a teenager working in a bar, everything I've done has been with people in mind.

Whilst I would say that I have a high degree of insight, I don't and never will profess to be all knowing in the field of human psychology, as one of my strongly held beliefs is that we are all on a lifelong journey of learning so to profess this would suggest that there is nothing more to know or learn!

This belief in human potential drives everything I do and is also at the heart of how I do and be in this world. As such the Adaptive™ is merely an approach rather than a fixed model of fact or one-size-fits-all solution. By an approach I mean a set of ideas or actions intended to facilitate exploration. To me an approach is just a way of drawing closer to the recognition of potential or moreover an access point aimed to enable movement towards realising potential.

I wanted to make my approach as adaptable as people are. No two days are really ever the same for an individual even though at times it may feel this way. Every moment brings new experiences and by virtue therefore every day brings a whole new set of learnings, conscious or unconscious.

As humans we are evolving constantly so I wanted to ensure that whatever I do facilitates, accelerates and liberates this evolution. A model is a representation of a system that allows for investigation of the properties of the system. Humans are not systems. Humans are living, breathing organisms of energy in movement consistently stimulated by and stimulating, the environment they inhabit. We cannot neatly box or package this up, it is just too limiting and inhibiting of human potential.

As an approach therefore I offer ideas that enable exploration of the uniqueness of each individual human or organism. I have facilitated with the approach now for a few years to accelerate and liberate. Now it's time to take it to the next level to use it more widely to assist social leaders in dealing with the difficult situation we now face with the highest levels of dependency and debt ever recorded.

I have already explained the primary concepts behind the approach in terms of the diamond structure facilitating oscillation, balance and alignment. In this section the four main components that complete the approach will be revealed.

Whilst reading this section I would encourage you to complete the reflection exercises as you go as they will expand your understanding and facilitate even deeper awareness of self.

Take it to the next level

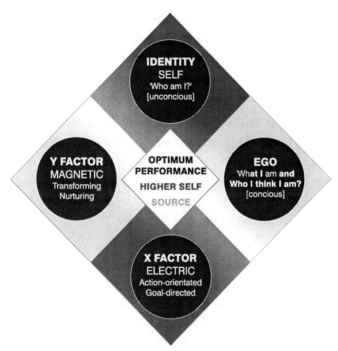

These are the four dimensions that facilitate the exploration of the approach. They consider the make-up of the unique individual being (be that an organisation or a person) in terms of its Identity (SELF), Ego (self) and Energy (Magnetic and Electric).

Energy

The world is revolving and evolving everyday, there is nothing static and by this I mean, motionless, still, inactive, for to be this way suggests that energy isn't present. We are a planet made of pure energy and that which has no energy field technically therefore, has no life.

Energy can be defined as the capacity for any physical system to perform. Energy exists in several forms such as heat, kinetic or mechanical energy, light, potential/stored energy, magnetic, electric, or other forms.

According to the law of conservation of energy, the total energy of a system remains constant, though energy may transform into another form. Two billiard balls colliding, for example, may come to rest, with the resulting energy becoming sound and perhaps a bit of heat at the point of collision.

Based on this analogy, I explored the potential within humans to use the synergistic power of their energies. When I refer to energy within humans I refer to the orientation of their energy in terms of electric and magnetic (or masculine or feminine), not specifically to the energies that provide our autonomic reflexes or physical ability etc...

As humans we are nothing other than amassed energy formed into matter. We are not machines made up of biochemical forms. Dr Bruce Lipton, biologist and author, says *"beneath the skin is a bustling metropolis of 50 trillion cells, each of which is biologically and functionally equivalent to a miniature human"* and each of which is approximately 100 trillion atoms. An atom is a fundamental piece of matter (anything that can be touched physically). Every object in the world is made of atoms including the chair you're sitting on.

Atoms are made out of protons which carry a negative charge, neutrons which carry no charge and electrons which carry a positive charge. In other words atoms are energy.

As energy beings therefore we are naturally connected without consciousness. We provide a charge wherever we are and that charge is transferred to another. You know when you've been with someone and you walk away feeling drained or with another you walk away feeling recharged and energised. We didn't get this language from nowhere!!

Energy has frequency and those frequencies resonate outward into the world around us, **projected and reflected**.

Tuned in or not the frequencies you surround yourself with affect your energy.

Tuned in they are honed to perfection. Think about your journey in a car when you tune into your favourite local radio station, a couple of kilo hertz can make the difference between hearing that station crystal clear or there being a distortion.

But as you drive further out of your locale, you start to go out of range of the station or frequency. The sound becomes distorted until such time as you lose it and suddenly another station has replaced it on almost the same frequency.

As humans we operate the same way and therefore we **cannot not** be in-fluenced. I deliberately separate the IN from Fluence as this makes the concept of influence even more powerful. Yes it is in the semantics again!

Fluence refers to the ease with which particles flow, and if you are IN fluence therefore you are in ease with the flow of particles. In other words you are vibrating energy that others around you will experience. Therefore by virtue of your mere presence you are influencing another.

This could lead us to believe that we gain our energy from others and so are reliant upon other humans to provide us with energy. Some do indeed, and some drain us of it. However, there is no limitation on energy, energy is infinite. We have an abundance. We just have to know how to tap the abundance such that it's not sucking the life from another!!

As atoms are the foundation of matter and they are mere energy then energy can be sourced from everything that surrounds us and most prevalently, energy is most abundant is in Mother Nature (e.g. trees provide us with oxygen). We have a constant stream of energy available to us when we decide to access it.

Energy guides our direction as humans in so many ways. How we think we feel and express that, is actually how we feel. I had a colleague once who used to respond to "how are you" with a sigh followed by "I'm tired". Raising this to his awareness and him choosing to respond differently had the most amazing effect in raising his energy levels. Another colleague told me the story of meeting a young man who said he hated mornings, without thinking she immediately responded saying: *"Oh God, that's awful, do you think as you're so young, you should get to like them?"* The young man thought about this for a few minutes and after a discussion he realised that this thought or belief was not serving him as it was sucking his energy in the mornings.

I've already said that words have an energetic value to them also, so we have an overwhelming amount of energetic influences on us on a daily basis that we are completely unaware of. Perhaps it is time to become aware and take ownership of choosing the influences we expose ourselves to and how we manage our own energy?

You have the power to decide to create or deplete your energy

We all have within our energy field both electric (masculine) and magnetic (feminine) energy. For simplicity, in the diagram I've 'labelled' these the X and Y factors. All of this is irrespective of gender. In fact in the spirit of seeing the world through an atom perspective, even genderless entities tend to display masculine and feminine energies. For example organisations, plants, cars, and even buildings. Subjective as these are or appear to be, have you ever named your teddy bear, your car, your home etc…

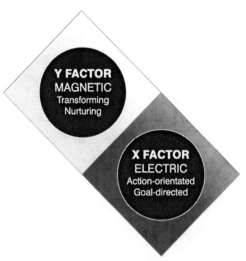

Ideally these energies would be balanced, which is not to say that each human would have a 50/50 balance but a balance that is appropriate to them personally. In my research I've yet to find any mechanism to measure the ratio in any one human. Yet actually I'm not sure this is required as you can see it displayed in full glory and in ourselves we know where we are weighted. Let me explain...

The Eastern description (in the symbol of the Tao) of yin and yang, now quite familiar in western culture, is a similar dichotomy.

The feminine or yin includes such attributes as receptive, creative, intuitive, imaginative, inward, sensitive, subjective, nurturing (see Appendix A for a more comprehensive description). In science this is considered to be a magnetic energy.

The masculine or yang includes such attributes as outward, action, firm, logical, strong, rational, dry, competitive (see Appendix B for a more comprehensive description). This is considered to be electric energy.

So if we consider a 'discovery', an 'invention' or a piece of 'art', it will have commenced in the magnetic/feminine energy field (creative). It will then be brought about into reality by the electric/masculine energy field (action). Thus the feminine initiates and creates, and the masculine energy implements into action and reality.

To function in the world therefore we absolutely need a balance of both energy fields irrespective of gender. This is not new information, we've known this for millions of years but in our recent history we seem to have forgotten it!!

Taoism goes back to fourth/fifth century before Christ. The Tao symbol, consisting of a circle divided in two equal portions each containing an element of the other, indicates that all of creation is composed of two energies held in harmony and interaction.

Science suggests that magnetic energy comes first, and then the electric; and appropriately adds that the electromagnetic wave should be renamed the magnetic-electric wave as the magnet is the source (as just demonstrated).

However, this is not how we live these energies. Psychology would suggest that in the first half of our lives we develop the energy associated most with our gender hence, men are predominately yang but contain a yin aspect. Women, while predominately yin, contain an element of yang. In later life, however, we are called to integrate the opposite energy, the anima (for a male the feminine component) or the animus (for a female the masculine component). This is a move towards wholeness.

As human beings therefore we are psychologically androgynous with dormant inner masculine and/or feminine energies awaiting development and we have capacity to tap into either energy at anytime. There is much debate about what the right level of balance would be, so for example would the perfect balance be 50/50 masculine/ feminine or would it be 55/45 and 45/55? My observation of human behaviour and the world we live in at present suggests that this is imbalanced and too far a leap to take at present given we've lost or have learned to repress so much of our feminine energy. Further perhaps an equal balance would negate the power of each?

My observation suggests that inherently we live our lives in a predominant energy, and then the balance ranges 60/40, 70/30, 80/20, depending on your openness and capacity for development. So you may well live predominately in masculine energy if you are male or feminine if you are female. But this could just as easily be masculine for a female or feminine for a male (which does not suggest or direct sexual orientation).

When we learn the capacity to develop both energies we open up new opportunities, experiences and perspectives in our lives.

Whilst some of the energies characteristics are stereotypical of gender they are not exclusive and when used effectively can offer the ability to adapt behaviour easily and without detriment when the need calls.

Reflection Time

An example of this was many years ago when I worked as a HR Business Partner in Professional Services. Ignorant of what I now know, my energy orientation was predominantly magnetic/feminine. I expressed very little electric/masculine and if you'd asked me about it I wouldn't have known what you were talking about.
Was I in for a shock…

I'd been chosen for the role because of my feminine energy as it required me to spot talent, groom it and accelerate it, coach very technical professionals on how to manage and motivate people, and manage all of the HR strategic and operational needs of in excess of 150 people. I was so excited by the role. As a professional service selling 'knowledge' I naively thought that people would be of the utmost value to the organisation. And to be fair, they were – intellectually.

Everyday the challenge "what is your evidence for saying that" came. Everyday I struggled to articulate in logical, systematic terms how I could spot talent. Everyday I tried to substantiate every word I said or evidence what I knew to be innately true. Everyday I worked with systems and procedures that were supposed to enable my role yet slowed me down. Everyday I was challenged with providing reports on progress of individuals when the proof was evidenced for the naked eye to see.

This makes it sound bad and for me at the time whilst I loved what I did, I was drained by the stark contrast of my feminine energy within an organisation brimming with masculine energy. I used to get so bogged down in the logic and stuck in the details. I remember once my colleague told me, "Paula, just play the game, don't get caught personally in the challenge, they aren't challenging you! They just need to see it for them." I now completely understand what she meant and thank my lucky stars for the learning, challenge and opportunity working with this organisation gave me.

Imbalanced Energies

Given that we believe in an electro-magnetic field (rather than a magnetic-electro one) it would suggest that primarily our masculine energy is our driving force. In chapter six we considered that 'everything is on-the-go'. We have become an action orientated nation that is only happy it seems when we're busy – doing!

Electric/masculine energy is action and goal orientated. It is ambitious, driven, competitive and individualistic. We just have to look around within our society to see the level of masculine energy in force. We have become a nation obsessed and defined by material possession. We are in a twenty-four hour domain, no room for sleeping. We never close, even on days such as Christmas Day you can still dine out, pick up groceries in your local garage or convenience store. At 3.00 a.m in the morning if you want food, alcohol, clothes or electrical goods there are plenty of 24 hour stores that will accommodate you.

Our nation crams every moment of every day whilst we hurtle ourselves from one place to another. Time, time, time. Pressure, pressure, pressure. Stress, stress, stress. If we make no space to just be, the net result is that we overextend our electric/masculine energy. Like everything when it is overextended or overwhelmed there are consequences. And the consequences are what we are seeing in our society. One that is driven by excessiveness, aggressiveness, blame, rigidity and has become dehumanised and impersonal. It is unsustainable and as a friend of mine once said, *"sets us up to fall like a bag of spanners"*.

This, for me, is why we're in recession. We have been unable to help ourselves slow down, take thoughtful considered decisions, access the human values of connection and love in the pursuit of success and materialism. We have brought this about ourselves! We have been both the cause and the effect.

The feminine/magnetic energy is about 'beingness' but as I've already highlighted we seem to have forgotten how to stop, be and live in the present (the gift). Either that or we've simply decided that to stop is lazy!!

Mother Nature is the feminine energy's best friend, she provides a stillness yet movement in her energy to allow and enable flow. A dose or two of this and you can unleash the artist within – we all have the capacity when we let it!

Conversely detriment will also result if we overexert our magnetic/feminine energy, which is about transformation, nurturing, creativity and the collective. I've already pointed out the consequences of over-nurturing in the opening chapter. Not only does dependency result, but we also have a sense of emptiness, despair, stuckness and over-indulgence!

Consider if you will for a moment the levels of staff turnover and burnout in professions such as health, caring, psychiatry/counselling and social work.

Reflection Time

I ran a workshop with about eighty social workers, which was designed to facilitate their development of solutions to implement the recommendations that arose from the Social Work Task Force report. I was met with a very heavy energy in a group of people who felt stuck, depressed and who found it difficult to express what they wanted focusing only on what they didn't want. I took a different tact and allowed them to become aware that their fear of change was keeping them stuck in the stuff they wanted rid of. They talked of the level of burn-out in their sector, the stress of caring for the people they worked with, the lack of sleep they experienced thinking about their clients. The helplessness they felt when things didn't go right and the levels of guilt and shame they experienced as a result.

In a similar vein, but with different constraints, I've met many teachers also in my time whose only ambition as a child was to be a teacher. They've studied and qualified and finally got into a teaching environment only to find the system (our education structure) does not allow for their feminine energy to be expressed unless they are working in early years. The masculine structure of the system stifling their creativity in delivering the education they believe children and young adults would benefit from, which is more experientially grounded than academic as it is now. There is also little room for individual nurturing in a class of thirty students.

Exercise Time

Go to Appendix A noting the descriptors of electric (masculine) and Appendix B for magnetic (feminine) energies. Evaluate the day you've just had (or day before). Was this a typical day for you? If yes, consider the descriptors to assess where your balance may lie. Continue this exercise for at least a fortnight to get a fuller picture of how you truly operate in the world.

> *"The more you lose yourself in something*
> *bigger than yourself,*
> *The more energy you will have"*

Norman Vincent Peale

EGO

Much literature is available from sociological, psychological, philosophical and other fields on the ego. My intention here is not to question any of this it is simply to offer a pragmatic perspective of ego in relation to the Adaptive™ approach.

What this literature and our language have come to offer in western society is a demonised perspective on what ego is. In essence though the word itself has a very simple definition, it has in no way the depth of negative connotations, which we have come to associate it with.

Ego by definition means *'a sense of own self-worth'* or *'your consciousness of your own identity.'* In other words every being that ever lived or breathed has an ego.

Why do we have this? To survive in the world of billions of people somehow we need to have a sense of our own individualism. Conversely and as importantly, our ego is what keeps us connected with other beings knowing that we are part of something larger and although our individualism is important it doesn't exists in and of itself, it exists only in relation to another.

In the first chapter I introduced you to a poem by John Donne which commences with the line *"No man is an island entire of itself; every man is a piece of the continent, a part of the main".* Our ego knows this inherently and its job is to embrace that connectedness to others whilst at the same time expressing the uniqueness of amassed energy that makes up each individual.

But because the ego only exists in relation to another, it compares. To compare is to judge. We must make judgements that keep us both safe in our connection to others yet at the same time retain individualism. A bit of a contradiction if not even an oxymoron!!! Bless the human race.

It is no wonder we get confused in life and lose ourselves or end up with an inflated or deflated sense of self.

This is why our sense of self must run deeper than our consciousness or self-conscious. According to research done by Dr Bruce Lipton (expressed in Spontaneous Evolution) the self-conscious mind is a small 40-bit processor that is the seat of cognitive thinking, personal identity and free will. As such this is the part of our mind that decrees our desires and intention hence taking the oxymoron to extreme he makes a joke of it. The joke being that this part of the mind *'imagines who we think we are'* but it only controls 5 percent or less of our lives.

When I read this first I was in disbelief because in my experience it plays such an enormously significant part in human life. However, I read further to reveal that in fact the unconscious is determining our lives 95 percent of the time, which means that our destiny is in the control of all the **"recorded programmes** *that have been derived from instincts and the perceptions acquired in our life experiences".*

In other words we're operating from the basis of everything that we have learned along the journey of life, everything that has subliminally been embedded. Just like the story of the psychiatrist in the US who subliminally programmed his clients to feel old and depressed and then young and energetic (chapter five).

And all the while all we are seeking is to remain connected to others with a sense of self in tact.

When Ego rules, humans get bruised

So if this is all that's running then we are genuinely living an illusion. An illusion based on everyone else's perception and interpretation of who we should be rather than self-directed sense of who I really am. In essence we fall into the trap of being 'what' everyone else needs us to be, all of the labels of 'what' I am rather than 'who' I really am.

The labels consume us and dictate how we should behave. So the mother who think she's a good or bad mother in comparison to what the label says she should be. The husband who thinks he's a good or bad husband according to what the label says he should be and what other husbands are like and what his wife's interpretation of the label is too.

The child who is told he is a good or bad child according to his teacher who compares him incessantly against other children in his class or his sibling who had been there before him.

We are constantly bombarded with what we should be. The perfect figure, the perfect face, the perfect job, the perfect house, the perfect family, the perfect marriage, the perfect holiday, the perfect car, the perfect clothes, the perfect image. The status, the positioning in society, the financial success all make up what the ego strives for.

Either that or it just gives up knowing it is unworthy in comparison to others, it is inferior and not now or never will be enough. Because it doesn't have the perfect anything, it doesn't have the status and doesn't know how to get it, or doesn't feel it has the resources that others seem to have.

Resentment and bitterness ensue on one hand, superiority and an inflated sense of worth to the world on the other hand.

Neither allows for the beauty of the continuum in between where there is no better or worse, no more or no less, no bigger or smaller, no taller or thinner, no stronger or weaker, no pretty and no ugly... and so on and so on.

In its external nature it is dependent upon the outside world for its nurturing and can often therefore find itself in a vulnerable position, exposed to the opinions, needs and sometimes callous nature of others. Its esteem can quite easily get bruised and battered so to counteract this it acts in a segregated manner i.e. its confidence shines in one area and has low esteem issues in another. This separateness, however, can weaken the fibre of ego and in turn present an inconsistent social identity, potentially creating mistrust.

Self-esteem is at the heart of all of it and if the pendulum is swinging then the individuals' sense of self is fragile, because they judge themselves by what's outside them rather than what's within. In this place the judgement is either favourable or unfavourable to make them feel either better about themselves or worse!

Here ego provides either an inflated feeling of pride in its superiority to others, or at least this is how it can appear. Likewise ego can provide a deflated image of itself and its inferiority to others. I quite often find clients saying things like *"I don't have the qualification to do that"* or *"... is better than me at that"* or *"I couldn't possibly think of presenting, my nerves would just crumble me"* and so on and so on. You get the picture and you've heard yourself at times put you down before you've even tried something. Sometimes this can be the ego's way of protecting its position or from exposing the real self and indeed the ego's fear of change.

A perpetual cycle on the swinging pendulum takes over life's journey. Learning is stunted as it is inhibited by the individual's sense of what's either possible or not. Hence the individual has now developed a sense of needing to be needed. When someone else needs them it boosts their sense of self, when no one needs them it deflates their sense of self. Everything is a direct dichotomy, nothing lives in between in the place of moderation.

In this place in ego we now need to hide the bits of us that we have come to know, based on our recorded-programmes, are unacceptable. We fear being judged if we let them out. We fear being rejected. We fear being isolated. Remembering the job of the ego is to keep us safe in connection to others, this is a rather futile place to be.

What we don't realise is that they leak out and others can still see them. But our minds fool us into thinking that it has control and we're playing a good game, acting the part really well and we're fooling everyone around us!

This is when life becomes a stage, and we become mere actors within, playing a part or role that some director has cast us for, based on a script that often someone else has written. The rules change everyday and in order to keep my job I must dance to the new tune, I must, chameleon like, keep morphing into the role. The role of mother, wife, husband, leader, follower, daughter, worker, community member, friend, colleague, neighbour, reader, writer, plumber, teacher... etc.

The ego seems to have fulfilled both its roles, it has kept us safe in connection to others, and in essence it has also kept it sense of self. But there are stings. Self in relation to others is not in relation to self! Also if I'm not connected to me, can I truly be connected to another?

Am I the person I present to the world?

My ego is the external presentation of self, that which is on display for the world to see. Hence it is seen by 'what I am/ do' rather than 'who I am'. It is action-orientated (utilising its masculine energy) as it visibly displays all of the nuances of our gestures, mannerisms, habits and general physiology. It is audible as you can hear the speech and tonality. The ego sets the stage for a person's social identity. The ego is the actor on stage.

As Gary Oldman (actor) put it: *"To be able to do this job in the first place you've got to have a bit of an ego."* So it has a very conscious positioning and is in control of how it acts. Ego enjoys and relishes in this control and constantly seeks it out. But another sting, when you have a need for control, control controls you!

However, as we've already seen, it is not in control of the stage and the other actors that occupy it. Therefore it is at the mercy of the shoulds, oughts, musts and expectations of its fellow actors (other humans) and the stage in general (social environment) to ensure that it fits into and relates to its environment. Isolation is not an option for the ego as it now relies on the external environment for its nourishment and validation. And again can something that is not connected to itself be connected to anything else?

The Ego's **worth** is measured by its material success or status. In response to the question 'what is your purpose in life', one client responded:

> *"As long as I look like I'm doing well that's all that matters, as in, I've got my apartment, my BMW and my own business and of course a good looking woman to share it all with."*

This client was living in ego, a rather unbalanced life and one which proved difficult for him to maintain without pain, hence his entry to coaching.

The ego's **worth** is evaluated against others in its immediate environment, its family, and significant others as well as by society in general hence the saying 'when in Rome do as the Romans do'. In the ego's need to belong it can find itself conforming and complying to the culture that surrounds it, hence ego is flexible, rational and objective in its approach. It is very much in touch with its perceived external reality. Much of the ego is lived in the masculine energy stream (electric).

But it is not all bad
EGO – Essence Glowing Outward

When we allow and when we develop wholly as beings connecting in with the recorded programmes we run, allowing ourselves to hear the messages our emotions and feelings offer and therefore knowing that inherently we are enough, we are acceptable and we are loving and lovable, the ego becomes our essence glowing outward.

Here ego can provide us the vehicle with which to navigate in this world, which at times can be violent, chaotic, challenging and demanding whilst also being beautiful and joyous. The vehicle protects the driver (our inner being/ Identity) and allows us to adjust to the conditions we find ourselves in – the many faces for the many places we visit or a mask for every occasion, or perhaps to not have to wear the mask at all!!

Reflection Time

Consider the last time that you blocked yourself and resisted a change, was it because of your ego or did you genuinely know that it wasn't right for you? If the answer is yes ego did rule, then you already know that you're on a journey to consciousness. If you've said no it was genuinely not right for you, read on to Identity and at the end of that come back to this question and reconsider.

Identity -Who are you?

When I engage with a client whether it's a group or an individual one of the first questions I ask is *"who are you"*?

Reflection Time

Take a moment now to consider this question
– Who are you?

How would you answer it? Write it down and
when you're done read on.

Identity – the who inside me

Our internal orientation is our Identity, this is our authentic and/or congruent self – the 'who' I am. As authentic implies the Identity is the true self underpinned by the consciousness of values, beliefs, passions, purpose, preferences and pure innateness. It is the inner core of our being and therefore offers up our emotional and relational esteem, which is derived internally from our individual and personal sense of worth.

As the ego plays the lead role on the stage in front of the world, the identity is the backstage player that supports the front stage actor, offering its inspiration of individualism and its DNA or Divine Natural Attributes (Dr Robert Holden – Success Intelligence) to the ego to enable it fully on stage.

It is the 'being' of the individual in preference to its counterpart 'doing' ego.

Therefore it provides the foundation and stability that the ego needs to function effectively without reliance upon the external world for all its validation or esteem.

As with ego, identity has aspects that could be considered positive or negative, although for me it is all in how you use it!

Its positive aspects are in knowing and understanding self, we become conscious and in consciousness we can create greater choice; in how much of the self is exposed; in how we live our purpose, passions, values and beliefs; in how authentically we choose to live; and therefore what environments will support our congruence. It provides us with the freedom to live rather than exist.

In Action

I've had many clients come through my doors feeling stuck. Having arrived at a place in their life that they thought was the 'be-all' place for them. It was what they planned for, what they believed they desired. Many highly successful but their success has come at a price and they know not what the price is or why they are paying one. Through coaching over a period of time clients eventually discover their purpose for being in this world, how they can truly contribute.

One such client, Tony (described in 'Survive in Action') found that some of what he was doing was very much right for him, but some wasn't. Tony began to exercise conscious choice and in doing so he's now re-channelled his focus at work and has a renewed sense of his role as a husband, father and friend. He has developed a really strong relationship with himself.

He is deciding what of who he is he can love. There are other parts of him he's yet to discover and other parts that he's yet to accept and therefore love. However, this is his journey and his process and he's enjoying the travel. Overall Tony has a renewed sense of self and in this heightened awareness state he now has the ability to give more to his family, his work and yet still has much left for himself.

Conversely identity's negative aspects are in 'Identity Conflict' i.e. when our differentiated self doesn't fit with the environment we find ourselves in and in remaining congruent with self we seem to enter conflict with others. This has been a constant in my work. As clients take on the journey to discovering who they really are they start to open their perspectives on life and in doing so they initially become more understanding and tolerant of others because they appreciate that they don't always see life the same way so take the time to open to a new perspective.

However, over time they can get a sense that actually where they are is no longer where they want to be. Colleagues, friends, family and loved ones don't want them to shift either, they want them to go back to where they were, as they were. It's all a bit too frightening. This is the point of tension – tension between the past, present and potential future. This is where many find their position so uncomfortable they recoil and go back to living a life that others perceive they should lead. But with encouragement they can push through and in the strength of their knowingness of self they can move beyond.

It doesn't always mean that they have to leave or lose people it merely means their relationships takes on a new level. But sometimes they do make the choice to move on and to lose or leave those that have been in their lives for some time. Merely because it is no longer where they want to be, but they are the owners of these decisions, no one else. They are doing it for them, no one else. And whatever their choice, it is always the right one for them, and therefore also right for others.

The second perhaps more difficult aspect of identity is that it is at our core and as such is the 'raw' me in all its fragility. There are times when this gets exposed unintentionally as the ego is unavailable to protect it. This can cause deep scarring.

In Action

Coming back to Tony again, he was working for an organisation that had held a dominant masculine energy along with an incredibly strong ego approach in the superior sense. Tony had found this difficult as much of the organisation's values and beliefs contradicted his own. He constantly felt stressed and drained. If he expressed opinion that conflicted with the leader he was shot down in flames and publically humiliated. Tony was metaphorically battered and bruised and for the most part because he was stripped of choice (or that's how he felt). To keep his high powered job, Tony had to be a 'yes man'.

Values evolve and develop over our lifespan

Over the past few years specifically I've been asking this question of anyone who'd care to engage:

Exercise Time

If asked to list your top ten values could you do it without thinking and as a stream of consciousness?

Secondly if asked to list your top ten beliefs again could you do that without thinking?

Before you read on, give it a go right now and see what happens…

I've been asking these questions because earlier we discovered that we have *'recorded programmes'* and these shape our values and beliefs. When I asked myself the questions many years ago I found it incredibly difficult to answer. I was puzzled at why something that only I could know was so difficult for me to either access or articulate. I observed myself for months and began noticing more and more. Each time I was faced with what seemed like a new one to me I'd write it down and note again when it manifested. At the end of the process I evaluated from the perspective of what was useful and what was not by asking the question *"does this serve me"*? In many instances it did in the past yet was no longer appropriate. Whenever the decision was that the value or belief was no longer serving me, I let it go and either there and then created a new one or allowed the new to emerge in the fullness of time and experience.

In the years I've been asking this question, rarely have I met anyone who has immediately listed off their values and beliefs. Generally the first question I get in response is, what's the difference between the two? Do you know?

In the opening chapter, we looked at values and beliefs briefly. There I offered examples of each and the story of the young boy called Tom to demonstrate them in action. Here

I wish to offer a fuller explanation to help differentiate and identify each further.

Beliefs use all our past based experience and what we've learned to drive us or to make decisions, which to a large extent are in the unconscious *'recorded programmes'*. Where as values allow us to move forward to consciously consider what we want to experience.

Beliefs are deeply rooted unconsciously, guide everything we do and rarely do we stop to consider the impact they're having and whether what served us 20 years ago continues to serve today.

Exercise Time

In response to my question I received the following email. See if you can spot the beliefs that underpin what is being said:

> *"...but it's good that these things are being talked and thought about. And believe me, I am thinking a LOT about the actions of 20 years ago, how they have led me to where I am today, and if my belief system then is still valid now (It's not – couldn't possibly be!)…*
>
> *"I am doing a degree, 1 year full-time, with a practicum next summer. It's gonna be tough, but it's EXTREMELY interesting. The ethics lecture is obviously in there for the potential bad apples who will take the information that they glean from this course and turn to the dark side..."*

What beliefs can you extract from this? Have a go before you read on…

Are there any values being expressed here? Again write them down where you perceive them.

Some of these are outlined in Appendix C which you can refer to at a later stage, to confirm your thoughts.

*"Whatever one believes to be true either is true
or becomes true in one's mind"*

John C. Lilly

In his book, *'Seat of the Soul'*, Gary Zukav tells the story of the nobleman who went to his mentor with a conundrum. The nobleman as part of his dress was required to wear a sword but as a peaceful man he increasingly found this more difficult, yet not to wear it in public would cause offense to his fellow citizens. He asked his mentor what he should do and he simply responded by saying: *"you will continue to wear the sword until such time as it is so uncomfortable you will stop."* That sounds so ridiculously simple yet it is actually how we live life.

In Action

One of my colleagues, a really ambitious lady studying for her degree, had so many plans for her life. She saw in her future a beautiful house, the most amazing wardrobe full of designer clothes, a good looking man at her side, success in her career (she planned to become a CEO by the age of 30), and finally after achieving all this she would have a family.

But at the age of twenty-two she found herself pregnant. Her life changed considerably as she decided to keep the baby. She did finish her degree afterwards and settled for a job that offered a level of flexibility that she needed as a mother. She and her partner settled down, but her hankering for all her plans never really left. She finally got a job that she enjoyed and that offered a little more flexibility and then suddenly found herself pregnant again!

She re-planned her life again but she was adamant that she was not giving up this job that promised her a glimmer of hope to rejoin the path she'd originally set for herself. She planned her maternity leave meticulously considering her financial situation and childcare arrangements. During her maternity leave she also married her partner.

She went back to work confused. A part of her was desperate to get back yet another and now seemingly more significant part of her wanted to be at home with her children. Suddenly the clothes, the career, the house, the success looked entirely different to her. Internally she was screaming with the levels of conflict she was experiencing that she just did not understand. Why could she not just get on with the job in hand, she knew it was for the best ultimately.

But it didn't work like that for her and after a couple of months she requested a shorter working week so that she could spend more time with her family and children. She reorganised her life to create the space. One external value that completely changed was her view of having a cleaner. When it was suggested to her she was appalled. She said: "My husband's family already think I'm above my station what would they think of that, and besides what kind of person would I be that I couldn't even clean my own house." It was suggested to her that she was merely being resourceful and that actually she was offering another employment where otherwise there would be none.

Ultimately she now works a shorter week, has a cleaner that not only cleans her house but irons too.
The time spent with her children is for playing and having fun doing activities that don't cost a great deal of money. Her wardrobe is what it is and she's not that bothered. She lives where she lives but loves her home, not her house. She still loves her job and puts everything of herself into when she is there.

Her journey was not without its challenge, disharmony, pain and joy. But her values have shifted. Old beliefs that no longer serve her have been released and new beliefs in the blessedness of family have taken over from her beliefs of success.

Exercise Time

What values have you changed in your lifespan?
How has this served you?

What beliefs have you let go of and what have you replaced them with?

Unearthing the unknown me is the Key

Taking time to be with self without distraction or allowing yourself to be an observer of yourself is crucial to getting to know you. If you wanted to get to know another person you'd spend quality time with them; you'd actively listen to what they had to say; you'd engage in conversation with them; you'd ask them what they enjoy, how and when etc... and you'd offer them love and affection.

Do you or have you ever done any of this for yourself, or are you like billions out there that would say talking to self is a sign of madness or at the very least taking such time is indulgent and therefore selfish.

There is no madness in talking to self contrary to what we may have been taught. Every person I've ever met has voices going on in their head, a dialogue constantly chattering away in their mind programmed by a lifetime of exposure to other people's belief systems and patterns of thought. When asked whose the voices are almost always their own voice is one of the voices speaking. This is normal and natural yet only as far back as 50 years ago, you could have been committed for saying such a thing. Now though talking to yourself is seen as the first sign of excellence! If you observe what you're hearing and take note you'd be amazed at what you could learn from yourself!

And in respect of indulgent or selfish, this couldn't be further from the truth. If you deny or simply don't explore parts of you, you deny the gifts of you, which in turn means you deny others the fullness of what you can offer. You are far more amazing than you know or think of, you have so much more to offer that you haven't yet even considered.

Being on Purpose

One further essential ingredient of identity is that it holds the key to your purpose for being on this plane of manifestation at this time.

Exercise Time

For what purpose are you on this earth?

What is it that you specifically have to contribute to the world in whatever way?

Why are you here now, in this era?

Do you ever ask yourself this and if you do and you already know all of this, is everything in your life aligned to this?

These are really big questions and ones that my clients are generally floored or overwhelmed by. Sometimes though, some can without hesitation express exactly what their purpose is and how they are living it, being it and offering it.

When you have this element, it is amazing how life just drops into place. Everything that you've experienced suddenly makes sense to you and all the pieces of the jigsaw of your life fall into place beautifully creating the whole picture. Now you are ONE.

From this place of knowingness you can live a life that is in complete authenticity. Every action, thought and decision are congruent throughout your entire body, soul and life.

Your purpose is your navigation system guiding you like a compass to where you need to be, what to do, how to do it and who to connect with along the journey (remembering your vehicle is your body and your ego).

Challenge will still enter, emotions will still roller-coaster, shift will still happen and knowing this, you will move through all with grace, ease and with a greater sense of love and belief for life.

The Balancing Act – Ego and Identity

When we understand the purpose of ego and identity we can begin to use each in a way that holistically drives the whole person to fulfilment of potential.

When both operate in harmony the ego becomes the vehicle to drive forth the personal self to enable a life that is lived for self, without detriment to anyone else. The result is pure inspiration to others and a heightened contribution to the space you occupy.

IDENTITY
SELF
'Who am I?'
[unconcious]

EGO
'What I am **and** Who I think I am?'
[concious]

In Action

Back to Tony. In all honesty he would tell you today not very much has changed in the organisation he was working for. However, in his realisation that he has choice because he has gained the balance between his ego and identity, he has been able to find a way of remaining in the organisation knowing that he is choosing to be there as externally it continues to serve his ego, but he gets his affirmation and validation from his identity and is no longer reliant upon his leader for this. And the funny thing is when Tony stopped judging his leader, he's found a new way of being with him and their relationship has gone from strength to strength.

Reflection Time

"If you want to reach a state of bliss, then go beyond your ego and the internal dialogue. Make a decision to relinquish the need to control, the need to be approved, and the need to judge. Those are the three things the ego is doing all the time. It is very important to be aware of them every time they come up."

Deepak Chopra

Operational Dimensions

This planet we live on, called the Earth or world is made up of about 6.8 billion individual human beings, each of us with our individualised uniqueness. We all have our own way of looking at life, the combination of many factors including our culture, nationality, history, environment, family, religion, media experiences etc...

Is it possible therefore that we would all have the same perspective in terms of how to live on and in this planet? To aid harmony, and to enable us to all to live together we therefore operate in three different dimensions and for the most part, like it or not, exercise choice or not, we do so concurrently. The three dimensions are:

- There is the inner self, the true me
- There is the outer self, the presenting me
- There is the social self, the me that operates within social/group/organisational context

And in the spirit of the power of three, there are three components at work in each of these sub-dimensions and they are: consciousness, sub-consciousness, and unconsciousness.

However, what differs between each dimension is the frequency with which we are in each. Let me explain.

Inner Self, the true me

In the first dimension we are in conscious-ness some of the time and aware through our body, emotions, and cognitions who we are being and whether we are being authentic or not.

Sometimes we are in sub-consciousness, where we have filed certain experiences or data (emotional, physical or cognitive) away but by paying attention to it can be brought into consciousness relatively easily. For example if I asked you to recall a specific telephone number you may not know this immediately (i.e. in consciousness), however, you can access it by focusing.

Finally for some of the time we are in unconsciousness, unaware of our motives for the physical, emotional or cognitive experiences and responses we manifest. This may be as a result of a difficult experience that we have chosen to hide deep within the recesses of ourselves for our own protection (or at least that's how we see it at the time). On a more conscious level it raises new values and beliefs for us the origin of which is not brought to consciousness.

This process of consciousness, sub-consciousness and unconsciousness can and has been described as Generalising, Deletion and Distortion in NLP (Neuro Linguistic Programming).

We have ownership in this dimension, limited only by self.

Outer Self, the presenting me

In second dimension we are in consciousness most of the time, aware of the image we are presenting, acting the role we have created for ourselves. Our actions are deliberate and therefore conscious.

We occasionally come across situations that cause us to examine the sub-conscious to source information that allows us to perform our role more effectively or to adapt ourselves to the immediate environment.

EGO
'What I am and Who I think I am?
[concious]

X FACTOR
ELECTRIC
Action-orientated
Goal-directed

On occasion we operate out of unconscious, but because we are performing, we are immediately aware we have acted out of character and move to correct it with consciousness.

Again in this dimension we also have ownership and we also have and can exercise some control, limited again only by self.

Social Self, the me that operates within a social/group/ organisational context

In the third dimension, we are acting in consciousness but within an energetic power that is greater than our personal energy. We find whilst we may be acting in consciousness we are not in control of self and find ourselves going with the higher energy. If you can imagine being at a football match and your team scores, you along with the entire stadium (aside from the away fans) jump to your feet and in harmony sing, shout, cheer and sometimes even kiss the person next to you – something you would never do and would be embarrassed by normally.

This is the power of the collective, of institution, the energy of the organisation. Have you ever found yourself working in an organisation knowing that something wasn't quite right, searching for a way to describe a seemingly intangible force? This is the collective power which takes on its own ego, its own identity and moves beyond the collective of the individual people. It is now a living, breathing organism all on its own.

In this dimension, we have ownership and only a little control, limited by energy levels both external and internal.

The Adaptive™ in Action

The Adaptive™ person is the combination of its identity, ego and energy orientation.

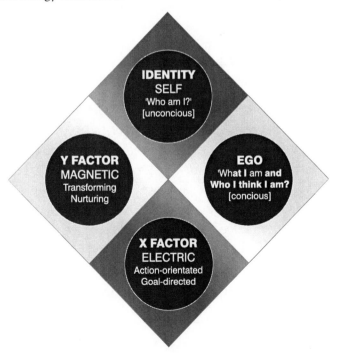

We've already described the benefits of combining masculine with feminine energies and also combining ego and identity. Now it's time to look at what happens when we put all of that together.

In Action

We've been using the example of Tony who had originally presented with a feeling of stuckness. To take this further the organisation that Tony was working in was incredibly masculine in its energy with little respect for the true energies of the feminine. Intellectually it talks about innovation, empathy with clients and authentic relationships. It also takes action to be innovative but its action is purely focused on competing with others in the sector, not on truly understanding what its clients needs are that they are currently not receiving. It talks about empathy but seeks to understand this through systematic analysis using logic and a rational approach. It talks about authentic relationships, yet lives in its ego. It is no wonder Tony was stuck!

The organisation is operating out of ego and in pure masculine energy. The result is that what it achieves on one hand is limited by its actions on another. Its employees only bring to the workplace what is deemed to be acceptable. They cannot bring all of themselves for fear that they will be isolated. They play the role that serves the ego of the organisation so they remain in conscious ego themselves all of the time.

Those with a feminine energy almost seem unwelcome. Individuals feel like they are being personally attacked by the challenges they receive and the more they experience this, the more withdrawn they become. The more they then need to move into an ego position to conform consciously to another energy so now not only are they out of balance with their energy they are out of balance with their identity. Feminine energy is needed and will be in existence in the organisation but hidden and obscured by the masculine energy that is visibly bringing it forward.

In everyday life we operate concurrently in each of the three dimensions of inner, outer and social self, through our conscious, sub-conscious and unconscious:

The difference between each is the depth and then frequency with which we spent time in consciousness and therefore the level of 'control' that we have in each. Whilst it would be boring (at least in my opinion) to operate in consciousness all of the time, it is highly useful to be able to exercise that choice, hence have ownership (rather than control) when you want to.

To enable us to operate effectively in these combined dimensions and therefore function authentically in the world amongst fellow human beings, without detriment to self or others, we need to bring about heightened level of awareness of self and also of others as this has the greatest impact in the third dimension and is the area where most humans get 'stuck'.

So for example I could be very comfortable in my inner self and have much of this on display in my outer self knowing that I'll not get caught short in unconsciousness very often. However, when faced with others and their individual uniqueness and perspective on the world, I am now challenged anew. I may not have experienced what I now face and therefore have little or nothing to draw from to enable my response. I am in a learning situation and as a learner how open am I? Do I fix myself to respond only from my way of seeing of the world or do I open to the possibility that there are other perspectives and whilst mine may be true for me, it does not necessarily mean it is true for others. Everyone has their own truth.

However, here we are not only dealing with individual truths, in the social self we are dealing with another higher energy, that of the group/organisation/institution. This organism has taken the collective of individuals and formed its own entity – an ego, identity and energy.

I now have to adapt not only to a differing perspective of another human or humans, but something beyond it that is intangible and for the most part implicit. Before I can do anything I need to know what it is and once I know then I have to find a way to be with it that doesn't compromise me.

I hear you say, *"this sounds very complex, time consuming and far too taxing, can I be bothered"* and I agree with you. So let's simplify it?

For argument sake, I'll call this intangible thing an energy. Choice, choice and more choice. I choose to be in this energy because it serves to lift me further. I choose to be in this energy and I choose to participate fully. I choose to be in this energy because it challenges my thinking and offers me the opportunity to broaden myself. I choose to be in this energy because it complements me.

I have not chosen to be in this energy so I will make a choice to exit it. I have not chosen to be in this energy so I will take what I need from it and leave the rest. I have not chosen to be in this energy so I will participate only to the degree that I feel comfortable. And so on and so on...

Choice arises as you have seen when you get conscious, because in awareness you know where your energies lie and in knowing this you develop confidence in whole self.

Knowing and understanding self and raising awareness does not give you full access to understanding others, but it does open the door to an awareness of how you are affected by others and therefore the ability to exercise choice about how you respond, becoming response-able. You can embrace fully, partially or remove yourself.

So the next time you're in work and find yourself conforming to a norm that no one seems happy with and no one knows why it exists such as *"well that's the way we've always done it"* you can choose to challenge it, you can choose to go with the flow of it, you can choose to learn from it, you can choose to embrace it. The point is you can choose...

Reflection Time

"I measure what's going on, and I adapt to it, I try to get my ego out of the way. The market is smarter than I am so I bend."

Martin Zweig

Précis

Energy: The orientation and flow of energy within humans (masculine or feminine).

Masculine Energy: (Electric) is action and goal orientated, determined and ambitious and when overused has negative consequences.

Feminine Energy: (Magnetic) is about beingness, transformation and nurturing. When overused has negative consequences.

Ego: Everything Good is Outside or Essence Glowing Outward, ego sets the stage for social identity and is the ultimate human element that ensures our continued connection to each other and humanity at large.

Identity: Becoming conscious of who we are at our core essence to allow us to create greater choices, providing us with the freedom to live rather than to exist.

Beliefs: Past experiences creating a guiding compass for orientating ourselves through life and the driver in making decisions.

Values: To move forward while conscious of what we want to experience.

The Adaptive™ Approach

CHAPTER EIGHT

Being Adaptive™

We all have resources beyond our wildest dreams, we just have not tapped them yet

All the resources we need are present already within us if we care to listen, to observe, to acknowledge and to accept. Life shows us in its infinite wisdom how to access them. Everyday, should we care to take the time to reflect, we bring forth new resources, new learnings, new ways of applying existing learning. We cannot not learn, but we can ignore the learnings and continue to repeat the same patterns, themes or mistakes over and over again. Each time we do life will offer us the same lesson again and again until we take notice and listen!!!

Every experience we have is learning, how we choose to apply that learning is another story! Life is like school really.

However, there is a subtle yet significant difference to school as we know it. School is where we go to learn the lessons, then take the test. However, in the school of life ('earth school'), tests come first and then hopefully we learn the lessons.

The lessons can only be learned when we take the time to reflect upon them and allow them to show us the resources we have and can access whenever or however we want. But if we're busy busy busy, doing doing doing all the time, how can we possibly reap the full benefits of all we have.

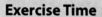

Exercise Time

What is the most important thing that has ever happened in your life?

What did you learn from that experience?

What specific inner resources did you use to deal with this?

How have you applied the learning or resources gained from this experience in other areas of your life?

Awareness is our Teacher and our Master

To raise awareness of self is to raise awareness of life, of love, of our fellow journey people and of the natural beauty and resource that Mother Earth offers.

In order to access this awareness we must allow the present to be. Instead though we spend much of our time either in the past or creating future history, in other words still in the past!!

The present offers us a stillness that makes the space for our hearing, our feeling, our being. No one can ever know you the way that you know you but without awareness others can see so much in you that you will never see in yourself.

So if you really want to be vulnerable then simply never raise your awareness!!

The present is a present, it's a gift and this moment will never come again. Although for some, time is a concept, it can only become a concept when it is being lived, and that can only happen if you live in the now. There is no other time!

> *"Realise deeply that the present moment is all you have. Make the NOW the primary focus of your life."*
>
> **Eckhart Tolle**

I watched an interview on the BBC with Charlie Stayt and Julia Roberts to promote the film *'Eat Pray Love'* in which Charlie asked if she felt her character represented a woman who was, as he termed it, 'navel-gazing'. Navel-gazing originates from the practice of omphaloskepsis, which is the contemplation of one's navel as an aid to meditation, but has subsequently been used as a slang term for someone who is self-absorbed and excessively introspective.

What does self-absorbed really mean and in whose opinion does introspection become excessive? Probably in the opinion of someone who is afraid to look inside themselves for fear that they may not like what they find!!

If we never stop to contemplate then how do we ever get to know self, conversely if we only look inward we fail to connect outwardly.

There is a balance to be struck. In no way can we be busy doing all the time, our body will take over and stop us, or we will overwhelm and become ill. In no way can we stand still either as the world continues to spin so we produce an opposite backward movement.

In Action

A gentleman, we'll call him Joey, who had been referred to me, recently engaged. In between our initial discussions and him attending his first session Joey had already started to observe himself reporting that for the first time in his life, he was really noticing his behaviour and responses.

In this first session Joey paid particular attention to his physiological responses to what we discussed or what his thoughts were. By the second session Joey had recognised that, for him, his body speaks his mind. He'd learned this by keeping a journal of his daily life and was discovering himself anew.

In the second session we played with this literalising what he was feeling so he could interpret the messages contained. Joey knew when he was moving into a denial, when he was feeling defensive or vulnerable, when he was joyful and curious and when he was excited or nervous. As he played with this physiology he suddenly stopped, tears filled his eyes and it was minutes before he found his voice. Joey said that he had experienced now the present moment in a way he had never done before. He was fully present in himself in the present and consumed in the now. The tears were of joy of finding a place of bliss that he never knew existed.

Joey had had many beautiful experiences in his life, including having been at the birth of his daughter, yet never had he experienced the power of the moment. Because never before had he let go to truly be here now. Up to this point Joey's mind had been what was present providing him with a constant chatter telling him about past and about future, analysing every thought that occurred. Now Joey was present in full mind, body, spirit and soul – here he was able to experience his energy and its power.

Joey practiced with this place even more and has reached the conclusion that he cannot 'make' anyone happy but he can share his happiness with others when he lets himself be in the fullness of his own greatness. Joey knows that every emotion, every feeling he ever experiences is a message. It's neither good nor bad, an upper or a downer, it just is an energy that offers him learning and can then move through him.

Joey has created an abundance of choice never before available to him. He no longer asks 'how' or 'why' as he knows these will inhibit his movement, and enable procrastination and fear to drive him. Joey now asks only one thing, what. His 'what' question directs and guides his choice and shows him the resources he has and when to use them and for what purpose.

Having this reflection means that Joey is in possession of the final element of the Adaptive™, the core of his being or his 'source'.

Exercise Time

Take a moment now to just be.

Experience your body, noticing where it is heavy, light, any tension or aches.

You don't need to do anything to change it, just noticing will release you.

Be an observer of the dialogue running in your mind, there is no need to participate and if you feel that you want to simply ask 'what next' until the thoughts slow down.

Make a pact with yourself to do this at least twice a day. It takes no more than a couple of minutes and is priceless for the levels of energy it offers.

It all boils down to four choices

I know where I first heard about these four choices because it resonated with me immediately, but I couldn't tell you the origin of the wisdom but it is one I feel compelled to share. For the many years I managed downsizes, re-engineering and closures I shared this wisdom with those affected and although in the moment some didn't quite get it, it stayed with them through the process and beyond giving them strength and courage.

In essence this life we live offers us four choices, in every moment, in every decision and in every connection we ever make.

The choices are:

- ▨ **Rebel/reject**
- ▨ **Resign/conform**
- ▨ **Walk Away**
- ▨ **Accept**

If you were to rebel or reject, imagine the emotions you would be experiencing. They would probably include anger, fear, pride, lust and have associated feelings of tension, angst and stiffness. Loss is the companion that will follow. Take a moment now to recall a time in your life when you experienced yourself rebelling or rejecting and notice what happens for you. It requires a lot of energy to rebel and reject, it is a place where energy is consumed and leaves you feeling drained and exhausted.

Is this a choice you need or want to make very often?

Now consider the emotions of resignation or conformity which would probably include apathy, a sense of 'what's the point', a victim-like hopelessness. The body experiences a heaviness, weight and depression. It feels like a burden that you have been left to carry without choice.

Again is this a choice that you would need or want?

Now think about walking away. It is likely that this choice has arisen because you've had enough or because it is just too much that you can't cope if you stay. The mixture of both emotion and feeling has a swinging pendulum effect that consumes energy from body, mind and spirit. A heavy heart results because no release can be found. Even when you walk away the memory remains to bring it life again and again.

Finally to accept is the choice of freedom. Acceptance liberates the connection to whatever is happening. It takes the depth of emotion out of the situation to allow for a dispassionate choice to be taken.

In Action

A friend of mine had been in a relationship for 14 years. Her and her partner dearly loved one another and desperately wanted to make things work but somehow no matter what they did they could not make the 'marriage' part of their relationship work. They had become like brother and sister, or companions who happily shared the same space.

My friend yearned for the intimacy of marriage and her husband yearned to give something he no longer felt. They were destroying themselves and each other.

He experienced a deep depression and she busied herself in life to avoid dealing with it all. Every now and again she'd have the most amazing outburst of emotion and threaten to leave him if he didn't change. He'd resign himself to her leaving him, feeling that he couldn't offer anything that would make the situation better. Yet neither actually did anything to follow through.

Over years of repeating this pattern both of them looked older than their age. Feelings of resentment, hurt, hopelessness, helplessness, bitterness, anger, rage and mistrust consumed their lives beyond their relationship together.

Eventually after one of her outbursts, he said he could no longer cope and would prefer to die than remain. He asked for a break and walked away to lick his wounds. She waited patiently believing that he would come back. Finally he came to her to say that he couldn't go back, he spat venom at how she'd been so dominant which had made him weak. Her dominance had forced him to live a life he hadn't wanted and had sucked the life out of him.

> *She resigned herself and took all the responsibility for his depression, for how lost he'd become in his life and for the overall failure of the relationship. Depression ensued for her.*
>
> *She worked with a coach and realised that all of the choices within the marriage had been based on the first three options of rebel/reject, resign/conform and walk away.*
>
> *Realising that she had responsibility only for herself she accepted that the relationship had ended and that she had actually unwittingly created this outcome. She accepted that it was right for her not to be in the relationship and that if he felt that it had all been her fault, then it was also right for him not to be in the relationship.*
>
> *Her acceptance led her to let go of all the hurt, anger, disappointment, sense of rejection and loss. She released herself and today she looks back on the relationship with much love and gratitude for all it taught her. In acceptance she has allowed herself to move beyond. She has an abundance of energy and a new found thirst of life, she realises that intimacy isn't the reserve of a marriage.*

Raising awareness of the choices we make paves the way for new possibilities to enter, new doors to open and an abundance of energy to follow. Whatever you focus on is what you get, so if you focus on rebelling you get more to rebel about. In acceptance you get to move through and onwards, there is no holding on to keep you back!

However you perceive your reality is your truth. If you perceive yourself as a victim then this will be your truth and situations and circumstance will provide you with the evidence to substantiate it. When you perceive your reality is that you are free to make choice, then choice will be your truth.

You can only know what you know and therefore only recognise what you know. You can choose whether what you recognise is narrowed or widened. When you take the space and time to get to know you more, then you widen your reality, truth and perception of self and therefore the world. And in doing so, you connect to your source, the deepest of your inner-self, or as I prefer, your higher self. Here there is only optimum performance because limitations cease to be as you realise that only you can impose limitations, only you can hold you back.

You have become Adaptive™. With peace in the knowledge that you are enough, you are connected without effort and when shit on from a great height you can offer out only love and light, purposefully using the richness of every experience to continuously evolve and grow.

In Stability I have the Ability

Where there is awareness there are strong foundations. This stability offers the ability to be adaptive to move within situations, align and connect with others wherever they may be at. It allows the flexibility to bend without compromise to authenticity or congruency.

In this place little can drain energy, little can hurt and even when it does it is short lived and merely just another learning.

The gift of this place is that the person can give without expectation or need. They no longer need to be needed or validated by others. The concept of giving and receiving merge as the individual realises it is merely energy that's being shared and in abundance.

Now the person is the change they wish to see and in being so, they offer permission for others to be and do the same. Their strong and solid foundation allows others to create, develop, evolve and be.

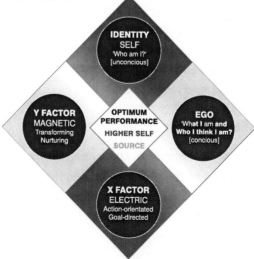

Reflection Time

In his inaugural speech, Nelson Mandela read a piece by
Marianne Williamson which reads:

Our deepest fear is not that we are inadequate. Our
deepest fear is that we are powerful beyond measure. It
is our light, not our darkness that most frightens us. We
ask ourselves, who am I to be brilliant, gorgeous, talented,
fabulous? Actually, who are you not to be? You are a
child of God. Your playing small does not serve the world.
There is nothing enlightened about shrinking so that other
people won't feel insecure around you. We are all meant
to shine, as children do. We were born to make manifest
the glory of God that is within us. It is not just in some
of us; it is in everyone. And as we let our own light shine,
we unconsciously give other people permission to do the
same. As we are liberated from our own fear, our presence
automatically liberates others.

The Adaptive™ person allows others to shine their light and
their power is boundless in authentic intent. Fear remains
and is harnessed usefully knowing it is merely another form
of guide.

Comfort zones pale as each day the Adaptive™ person seeks
to expand further and further feeling their fear in a way that
energises them further still.

Sympathy transcends to empathy and compassion for
everything and everyone. The Adaptive™ person feels the pain
and can be in it with another, not needing to make it better for
them, just holding and allowing the space for the other to be.
This means they don't feel that they have to give their energy
away because it is universal and doesn't belong solely to them.

Reflection Time

...I want to know if you can sit with pain, mine or your own,
without moving to hide it or fade it or fix it.

I want to know if you can be with joy, mine or your own,
if you can dance with wildness and let the ecstasy fill you to
the tips of your fingers and toes without cautioning us to be
careful, to be realistic, to remember the limitations of
being human.

It doesn't interest me if the story you are telling me is true.
I want to know if you can disappoint another to be true to
yourself; if you can bear the accusation of betrayal and
not betray your own soul; if you can be faithless
and therefore trustworthy.

except from 'The Invitation' by **Oriah Mountain Dreamer**

A place of peace and trust overtakes, allowing them to see the beauty in all others without recoiling to protect themselves. From here they are able to ask for help without feeling weak or vulnerable to seal the bond between giving and receiving.

The Adaptive™ person lives wholly, completely and fully in the knowledge that they are the creator of their own destiny. They have choice available to them always, and every choice they make leads to more learning and more choice.

Reflection Time

The Universe does not burden you with a destiny it provides
you with potential. How much potential you realise depends
on the choices you make. At each moment you are given an
opportunity to choose, what you choose leads you to more
choices. Each choice leads to yet more choices.

Gary Zukav

The Adaptive™ person realises they have only one job in life and that's to evolve to be the very best they can be. This is their full-time professional career.

Précis

Awareness: liberates to allow for the creation of new possibilities, thus allowing energy to flow.

Four choices:

- **Rebel/Reject:** Either one is a deeply painful emotional experience, thus often leading to physical or mental fatigue.

- **Resign/Conform:** A sense of hopelessness.

- **Walk away:** Leaving one with a sense of bitterness, anger or helplessness.

- **Accept:** The ultimate choice that offers freedom and release of painful emotional burden.

- **Choice:** creates choice.

Being Adaptive™

CHAPTER NINE

The Adaptive™ *Social Leader*

Your journey compels your teaching

No individual ever cannot not influence.

So as a leader particularly in the social sector I'm absolutely positive you would want to influence for the best and most productive possible outcomes. And those outcomes would be to further society as a place where respect, equality and parity lives and breathes in the widest sense possible, where every individual, in awareness creates the opportunity to live the life that is appropriate to them.

You are a role model to this. Your journey automatically shows others the way, it compels and is your teaching and as the Buddhist proverb suggests, "when the student is ready the teacher appears" yet likewise when the teacher is ready the student appears.

As a leader you are special yet no more or less so than anyone else as you recognise that you have as much to learn as you do to teach. You appreciate and acknowledge both the student and teacher within and remain open always in everything you do.

From here your influence is boundless and you are no longer so removed from the person or people you are leading your organisation to serve. As both the learner and teacher you have the ability to touch and feel that which your organisation is there to serve and you know that if one falls, all fall.

So you are on and in purpose and everything you do, say and be are aligned to this purpose. Likewise you recognise and appreciate the entity and organism that is the organisation you lead, and allow the fullness of its individuality and uniqueness to shine without tainting it to be a clone of you.

Like any individual being, you nurture and encourage the essence of your organisation to evoke its greatness and allow it too to find its purpose and align all its beingness with that purpose.

You and the organisation are now being the change you wish to see in the world, lighting the way for others to shine too.

You know that you are the extent of your limitations and that nothing outside can stop you without your permission. You trust that whilst authentically on purpose, that which you and the organisation needs to fulfil its purpose will be provided, you no longer need to be dependent upon others or external factors.

You are not attached to a plan or what the Government say or do or anything fixed or rigid that will hold you back. You are led by the people your organisation serves rather than by what you think you can or should offer, or what the funding allows you to offer.

You see through and beyond the presenting issues to facilitate solutions that serve to enable. And because you can see through and beyond, so can the staff within and therefore so can those you serve.

You are the Role-Model of Empowerment

Empowerment, particularly within the social sector is a rather overused word that actually, as has been seen by the contents of this book, is little understood.

When we truly empower those we are there to serve, we no longer need to serve them. Our role becomes one of facilitation and when we are done facilitating we make ourselves redundant and this is forever our intent if we are to respect the process of empowerment and belief in the capacity of those we serve to become empowered.

From here you will never condone disablement or dependency ever again and you will recognise its characteristic long before it becomes evident to others. You and your organisation will be full of and surrounded by 'can-do' people who share your purpose, share your inherent values, beliefs and the capacity of humankind.

Your influence precedes you and your presence is immense, filled with peace and strength. Once you've touched someone they will never forget, neither will they ever idolise you because you will have met them on the same level without intimidation, power or awe, you will have influenced them to seek within what they see out with.

The Tipping Point is here – the world has changed

You know that we have reached the point where you have to step completely into yourself and be in the fullness of your greatness. You have a crucial role to play in this world and you can no longer wait for someone else to do it.

Reflection Time

When I was a young man, I wanted to change the world. I found it was difficult to change the world, so I tried to change my nation.

When I found I couldn't change the nation, I began to focus on my town. I couldn't change the town and as a middle-aged man, I tried to change my family.

Now as an old man, I realise that the only thing I can change is myself, and suddenly I realise that if long ago I had changed myself, I could have made an impact on my family. My family and I could have made an impact on our town. Their impact could have changed the nation and I could indeed have changed the world.

Changing the world commences with changing self and from here we have ample capacity to influence the change we wish to see in the world. When you believe in you, you believe in the capacity of any one single person to create the life they want to lead. You are merely a fellow-journey traveller that lights the way, shines the light and gives permission for the others to find within them the strength and courage they need to travel beyond you.

When we take our power back we show others the ability to take their power too. If we don't we will continue to destroy the very essence of humankind. As an energy being you are connected to all other living forms. It is incumbent upon you to love yourself and when you do, you cannot not love another, as you and they are the same. And when more leaders and individuals like you within the world find this place of love, peace will reign, harmony will be our guide, words like equity will no longer need a place in our language.

A Call to Action

You already know you were born to make manifest the best of you. Your full-time job in this life is to evolve to be the best you can and in doing so, inspire, influence and model the way for others.

As a human your ego will continue to tell you that you need to be needed yet balanced by your energy and identity and in complete awareness you can harness this connection usefully and show others how to.

Start your own evolution not revolution. We don't need any big-bang, there are no fanfares and no fireworks. There is the steady, strong, consistent, quietly determined and unassuming you that forges your own way in this world, in the authentic desire to contribute fully to the world. And not because you know, but because you are naturally connected to all other life forms, when they hurt you hurt and when you light up they light up.

Be the light that shows others the way

Précis

Social Leader's awareness of self: The very essence of a role-model.

Empowerment: is to meet on an equitable level, one that creates respect and harmony from both teacher and student.

X Factor
Masculine Electric Energy

In Balance

X FACTOR
ELECTRIC
Action-orientated
Goal-directed

**Out of
Balance**

In Balance	Out of Balance
Objective	Complacency
Directed	Righteousness
Ordered	Dominant
Rational	Aggressive
Logical	Rigidity
Concrete	Excessive
Decisive	Rough
Factual	Individualism
Reasoning	Singular
Cognitive	Territorial
Systematic	Closed
Mechanical aptitude	Blame
Cause/effect	Impersonal
Judgemental	Un-sensitive
Linear expression	Insensitive
Independent	Dehumanising
Determined	Melancholic
Assertive	Expense of what's
Focused	life giving
Firm	
Drive	
Masterful	
Ambitious	
Exclusive	
Initiative	
Competitive	
Risk-taking	
Strong	
Honour	
Straight-forward	
Powerful	

Y Factor
Feminine Magnetic Energy

In Balance

Y FACTOR
MAGNETIC
Transforming
Nurturing

Out of Balance

Process-orientated
Methodical
Abstract
Relational
Spontaneous
Inspiring
Exploring
Intuitive
Innovative
Creative
Thinking
Flow
Responsive
Receptive
Participative
Collaborative
Conversational
Consulting
Conciliatory
Inclusive
Sharing
Accommodating
Adaptable
Flexible
Yielding
Embracing
Giving
Sensitive
Trusting
Empathic
Emotional
Vulnerable
Mischievous
Concern for distress

Compliant
Moodiness
Vague/diffuse
Despair
Emptiness
Depression
Fear of change
Stuck
Possessiveness
Destroying

Identifying Values and Beliefs

Exercise

What are the values and or beliefs being expressed in this excerpt:

> *"...but it's good that these things are being talked and thought about. And believe me, I am thinking a LOT about the actions of 20 years ago, how they have led me to where I am today, and if my belief system then is still valid now (it's not - couldn't possibly be!)...*

> *"I am doing a degree, 1 year full-time, with a practicum next summer. It's gonna be tough, but it's EXTREMELY interesting. The ethics lecture is obviously in there for the potential bad apples who will take the information that they glean from this course and turn to the dark side..."*

Here are some examples, there are plenty more that can be read too and the individual concerned may see even more...

Values	**Beliefs**
Discussion	*Talking is good*
Education	*Thinking provides answers*
Time to think	*Belief 'system' drives me*
Reflection	*Belief 'system' may not be valid*
Learning	*Doing a degree is tough*
The symbolism of a degree	*Information can be dangerous*
	There are bad people in the world i.e. good/evil and dark/light exists

Throughout her life Paula McCormack's passion for organisational, community and individual development has driven her every movement and spoken word.

Deliberately to understand the world around her, Paula has worked across corporate, private, public and third sectors. She's had the benefit of doing this in both thriving and recessional economic environments and experienced and observed the different behaviours these sectors provoke and promote and the behaviours that rise in the varying economic environments.

As such she has taken keen note of the impact of Government policies, approaches and general politics on all of the sectors, economic environments and therefore society and its citizens.

Twenty years on she has taken all of her wisdom gained to develop her personal approach to working with people, which she has called 'The Adaptive Approach'.

A lifelong student of learning Paula finds a continual source of inspiration her own personal development and experiences. Alongside her experience in the field of Human Resources and Development (HRD), Paula is a qualified NLP Practitioner, Hypnotherapist and Counsellor, an Accredited MBTI®, FIRO-B, 16PF and HAY Emotional Intelligence Practitioner, a Chartered Member of the Chartered Institute of Personnel & Development and holds a BA (Hons) Business Studies and PG in Strategic HR Management.

Lightning Source UK Ltd.
Milton Keynes UK
UKOW030619190712

196224UK00003B/7/P